OMNIBUSES AND CABS

# OMNIBUSES AND CABS

*THEIR ORIGIN AND HISTORY*

BY

HENRY CHARLES MOORE

*WITH THIRTY-ONE ILLUSTRATIONS*

First published by Chapman & Hall Ld. in 1902.
Republished by Adam Gordon in 2002.

A catalogue entry for this publication is available from the British Library

ISBN: 1874422338

Publication no.35

Published in 2002 by Adam Gordon,
Kintradwell Farmhouse, Brora,
Sutherland, KW9 6LU
Tel: 01408 622660

Printed by Halstan & Co. Ltd.,
Plantation Road, Amersham,
Buckinghamshire, HP6 6HJ
(Print run limited to 500 copies)

 I am most grateful to Dave Bubier of The Omnibus Society for his various researches. His recollection was that Moore was involved with cabs, possibly with the Scotland Yard Carriage Office, and wrote the book in retirement. One of Bubier's correspondents however believed he was a journalist/writer, but not in the cab trade. It appears Moore wrote a number of books between the 1890's and 1916, one of which was about the Chalfonts and Gerrards Cross. A Bucks Directory of 1907 confirms that Moores were landowners in Chalfont St. Peter and Gold Hill. In an attempt to pursue this line I did some research in the area with no result, and enquiries of the Special Studies section at Aylesbury Library failed to reveal anything more on H. C. Moore. I would naturally be very pleased to hear from anyone who can throw any light on the author.

Adam Gordon, December 2001

# NOTE

It is with great pleasure that I acknowledge my indebtedness to Mr. George A. Glover, who kindly placed at my disposal much valuable information concerning the early history of omnibuses and cabs, and several rare pictures, which are now reproduced for the first time.

I desire, also, to thank Mr. G. A. Thrupp, the venerable author of "The History of the Art of Coach-Building," for permitting me to have access to his interesting collection of illustrations of vehicles, and to reproduce several engravings dealing with the subject of this book. For a similar courtesy I am greatly indebted to the Worshipful Company of Coach Makers and Coach-Harness Makers.

H. C. M.

London,
*August* 23, 1901.

# CONTENTS

## PART I—OMNIBUSES

### CHAPTER I



### CHAPTER II



### CHAPTER III

## CHAPTER IV



## CHAPTER V



## CHAPTER VI



## CHAPTER VII

## CHAPTER VIII



## CHAPTER IX



## CHAPTER X



## CHAPTER XI



## CHAPTER XII

# PART II—CABS

## CHAPTER I



## CHAPTER II



## CHAPTER III

CHAPTER IV



CHAPTER V



CHAPTER VI



CHAPTER VII

# LIST OF ILLUSTRATIONS

# PART I

## *OMNIBUSES*

# OMNIBUSES AND CABS

## CHAPTER I

*Carrosses a cinq sous* invented—Inauguration ceremony—M. Laffitte's omnibuses—The origin of the word "omnibus" as applied to coaches.

Omnibuses, under the name of *carrosses a cinq sous*, were started in Paris in 1662. The leading spirits in this enterprise were the Duc de Rouanès, Governor of Poitou, the Marquis de Sourches, Grand Prévôt, the Marquis de Crénan, Grand Cup-bearer, and Blaise Pascal, the author of "Lettres Provinciales." The idea was Pascal's, but not being sufficiently wealthy to carry it out unaided, he laid the matter before his friend the Duc de Rouanès, who suggested that a company should be formed to start the vehicles. Pascal consented to this being done, and the Duc de Rouanès set to work at once to prevail upon members of the aristocracy to take shares in the venture. The Marquis de Sourches and the Marquis de Crénan he induced to take an active part in the management and, best of all, he obtained from Louis XIV. a decree authorising the establishment of *carrosses a cinq sous*. Seven vehicles to carry eight passengers each, all inside, were built, and on March 18th, 1662, they began running. The first one was timed to start at seven o'clock in the morning, but an hour or two earlier a huge crowd had assembled to witness the inauguration ceremony, which was performed by two Commissaires of the Châtelet, attired in their official robes. Accompanying them were four guards of the Grand Prévôt, twenty men of the City Archers, and a troop of cavalry. The procession, on arriving at the line of route, divided into two parts, one Commissaire and half of the attendants proceeded to the Luxembourg, and the others to the Porte St. Antoine. At the latter place three of the two-penny-halfpenny coaches were stationed, the other four being at the Luxembourg. Each Commissaire then made a speech, in which he pointed out the boon that *carrosses a cinq sous* would be to the public, and laid great stress on the fact that they would start punctually at certain times, whether full or empty. Moreover, he warned the people that the king was determined to punish severely any person who interfered with the coaches, their drivers, conductors, or passengers. The public was also warned that any person starting similar vehicles without permission would be fined 3000 francs, and his horses and coaches confiscated.

At the conclusion of his address the Commissaire commanded the coachmen to advance, and, after giving them a few words of advice and caution, presented each one with a long blue coat, with the City arms embroidered on the front in brilliant colours. Having donned their livery, the drivers returned to their vehicles and climbed up to their seats. Then the command to start was given, and the two vehicles drove off amidst a scene of tremendous enthusiasm. The first coach each way carried no passengers—a very unbusiness-like arrangement—the conductor sitting inside in solitary state. But the next two, which were sent off a quarter of an hour after the first, started work in earnest, and it need scarcely be said that there was no lack of passengers. The difficulty experienced was in preventing people from crowding in after the eight seats were occupied. At the beginning of every journey the struggle to get into the coach was repeated, and many charming costumes were ruined in the crush. Paris, in short, went mad over its *carrosses a cinq sous*, and the excitement soon spread to the suburbs, sending their inhabitants flocking to the city to see the new vehicles. But very few of the visitors managed to obtain a ride, for day by day the rush for seats became greater. The king himself had a ride in one coach, and the aristocracy and wealthy classes hastened to follow his example, struggling with their poorer brethren to obtain a seat. Many persons who possessed private coaches drove daily to the starting-point and yet failed to get a ride in one for a week or two.

Four other routes were opened in less than four months, but at last the fashionable craze came to an end, and as soon as the upper classes ceased to patronise the new coaches the middle and lower classes found that it was cheaper to walk than to ride. The result was that Pascal, who died only five months after the coaches began running, lived long enough to see the vehicles travelling to and fro, half, and sometimes quite, empty.

For many months after Pascal's death the coaches lingered on, but every week found them less patronised, and eventually they were discontinued. They had never been of any real utility, and were regarded by the public much in the same light as we regard a switchback railway.

After the failure of the *carrosses a cinq sous*, a century and a half elapsed before vehicles of the omnibus class were again tried in Paris, but one or two feeble and unsuccessful attempts to start them in England were made in the year 1800. A vehicle with six wheels and drawn by four horses was the most noticed of these ventures.

In 1819 Monsieur Jacques Laffitte, the banker-politician, who became, later, the Minister of Louis Philippe, introduced the vehicles now called "omnibuses" into Paris. They carried sixteen or eighteen passengers, all inside, and the fare was twopence halfpenny from one side of Paris to the other. From the day that they began running they were highly successful, and the first year's profits, it is said, repaid the outlay.

Monsieur Laffitte must not, however, be given the credit of applying the name "omnibus" to the vehicles which he introduced, for it belongs to Monsieur Baudry, a retired military officer. In 1827 Baudry was the proprietor of some hot-water baths in the suburbs of Nantes, and for the convenience of his patrons ran a vehicle at fixed hours to and from the town. This coach, which was similar in build to the Parisian ones, he named the "Voiture des Bains de Richebourg," but quickly came to the conclusion that the title was too long, and therefore endeavoured to think of a more suitable one.

It happened that just at that time a local grocer named Omnès caused considerable amusement in the town by painting over his shop "Omnès Omnibus." No sooner did Baudry see this than he declared that he had found the very word which he required, and straightway renamed his vehicle "L'Omnibus." Later, he started lines of omnibuses at Paris and Bordeaux, but they were not very successful, and the severe winter of 1829, which made forage very dear and the streets almost impassable, ruined him completely and drove him to commit suicide. But before he died he had made the word "omnibus" familiar to Parisians. Many of the vehicles belonging to other proprietors bore the inscription "Enterprise Générale des Omnibus," which, while not making people believe that the coach so inscribed was one of Baudry's, ensured its being called an Omnibus.

# CHAPTER II

George Shillibeer introduces omnibuses into England—The first omnibus route—Shillibeer's conductors defraud him—His plans for preventing fraud—An omnibus library—Shopkeepers complain of omnibus obstruction.

LAFFITTE'S omnibuses were so exceedingly well managed that they continued to prosper in spite of the many new lines started in opposition to them. With a view to maintaining the superiority of his omnibuses over those of his rivals, Laffitte decided to have two vehicles built which should eclipse in comfort and appearance any others on the streets. He gave the order to Mr. George Shillibeer, a well-known Parisian coach-builder. Shillibeer had been a midshipman in the British Navy, but quitted the service and went to Hatchett's, in Long Acre, to learn coach-building. Later, he started business for himself in Paris, and as English carriages were then becoming very fashionable, he met with considerable success, and built carriages and coaches for the most influential men of the day.

While executing Laffitte's order it occurred to Shillibeer that he might, with considerable advantage to himself, start omnibuses in London. He decided to do so, and, disposing of his business, returned to London and took premises at Bury Street, Bloomsbury, whence he made it known that he was about to introduce "a new vehicle called the omnibus." The word "omnibus" was received with marked disapproval by every person to whom Shillibeer spoke concerning his new venture. "If one vehicle is to be called an omnibus, what are two or more to be called?" people said to him.

"Omnibuses," Shillibeer replied promptly, but his questioners were horrified, and to their dying days preferred to call them "Shillibeers." Some people called them "omnis," and Mr. Joseph Hume, speaking years later in the House of Commons, created much laughter by referring seriously to the vehicles as "omnibi."

The route which Shillibeer chose for his first omnibus was from the Yorkshire Stingo at Paddington, along the New Road to the Bank. The New Road was the name by which Marylebone, Euston and Pentonville Roads were then known.

Three or four short-stage-coaches had been running on that road for many years, but as they took three hours to get from Paddington to the City, and charged two shillings for outside seats and three shillings for inside ones, they were not patronised by able-bodied people, who usually preferred to walk. Moreover, the short-stage-coaches were uncomfortably loaded with luggage, which they collected and delivered every journey.

On the morning of July 4, 1829, Shillibeer's two new omnibuses began to run. A large crowd assembled to witness the start, and general admiration was expressed at the smart appearance of the vehicles, which were built to carry twenty-two passengers, all inside, and were drawn by three beautiful bays, harnessed abreast. The word "Omnibus" was painted in large letters on both sides of the vehicles. The fare from the Yorkshire Stingo to the Bank was one shilling; half way, sixpence. Newspapers and magazines were provided free of charge. The conductors, too, came in for considerable notice, for it had become known that they were both the sons of British naval officers—friends of Shillibeer. These amateur conductors had resided for some years in Paris,

SHILLIBEER'S FIRST OMNIBUS.

and were, therefore, well acquainted with the duties of the position which they assumed. The idea of being the first omnibus conductors in England pleased them greatly, and prompted them to work their hardest to make Shillibeer's venture a success. They were attired in smart blue-cloth uniforms, cut like a midshipman's; they spoke French fluently, and their politeness to passengers was a pleasing contrast to the rudeness of the short-stage-coach guards—a most ill-mannered class of men.

Each omnibus made twelve journeys a day, and was generally full. So great a success were they that the takings averaged a hundred pounds a week. Nevertheless, Shillibeer had much to contend with. The short-stage-coach proprietors, disliking competition, endeavoured to incite the populace against Shillibeer by declaring that he was a Frenchman, and ought not to be allowed to run his foreign vehicles in England. Moreover, the aristocratic and wealthy residents of Paddington Green objected strongly to the omnibuses coming into their select neighbourhood, and petitioned the local authorities to prevent their doing so. And when they found that their endeavours were futile, they declared solemnly that Paddington Green was doomed. If they saw the neighbourhood to-day, they would consider, no doubt, that their prophecy was fulfilled, although, as a matter of fact, it was railways and not omnibuses that, from a residential point of view, ruined the neighbourhood. But the threatened doom of Paddington Green did not deter the sentimental poke-bonneted young ladies, who resided in the charming suburb, from spending a considerable amount of their time in watching the omnibuses start. In the middle of the day many of them were in the habit of taking a ride to King's Cross and back, for the sole purpose of improving their French by conversing with the conductors. That praiseworthy amusement was short-lived, however, for as soon as the omnibuses were in good working order, the gentlemen-conductors relinquished their posts and were succeeded by paid officials.

The new conductors were dressed in dark velvet suits, and as far as politeness was concerned were all that could be desired. Unfortunately they became possessed of the belief, not yet quite extinct, that to rob an omnibus proprietor was no sin. The amount of money handed in to Shillibeer grew less daily—a very suspicious decrease, considering that people living on the road which the omnibuses travelled declared that the vehicles were as well patronised as ever. Shillibeer therefore made arrangements with various trustworthy people to ride in his omnibuses, as ordinary passengers, and check the number of people carried and the amount of fares which they paid. For a few days every journey that the omnibuses made there was a male or female passenger watching the conductors, and from their reports Shillibeer discovered that the two men were, between them, robbing him to the extent of £20 a week. This was corroborated by the conductors themselves, whose style of living had become decidedly luxurious. In their time of affluence they did not forget their poorer friends, and one night, after work was finished, they treated a number of them to a champagne supper at the Yorkshire Stingo. The whole party became hilariously drunk, and while in that condition the hosts threw discretion to the winds, and bragged loudly that they made £10 each a week out of the omnibuses, in excess of their pay.

Among their guests were detectives employed by Shillibeer, who repeated the confession of fraud to their employer, with the result that the first professional omnibus conductors were discharged. Shillibeer's leniency, due to his anxiety not to have his omnibuses mixed up in any scandal, encouraged succeeding conductors to steal. Shillibeer was at his wits' end what to do, when a man called on him with a patent register guaranteed to put a stop to the conductors' pilferings. The register was designed to be placed underneath the omnibus, and people entering or leaving the vehicle trod on a plate fixed in the step, the register recording every person who stepped upon it. Shillibeer liked the idea, and bought one of the registers on the condition that the inventor acted as conductor until its reliability had been proved thoroughly.

For two weeks everything went well, and the conductor was anticipating an order for a second register, when a gang of men, in sympathy with the discharged conductors, attacked the omnibus while it was standing outside the Yorkshire Stingo, smashed the patent register with sledge-hammers, and half murdered its inventor. Shillibeer, who had paid £300 for the demolished register, did not order another one to be made, but tried a new and less expensive check, which was in use in the Paris omnibuses. A specially made clock was fixed in a prominent position in each omnibus, with a notice beneath it informing the public that it was the conductor's duty to move the hand a certain distance whenever a passenger entered, and requesting that any neglect of that duty should be reported to the proprietor. But, in spite of that appeal, the conductors neglected persistently to act according to instructions, and not one report of their breach of duty was ever received by Shillibeer from an ordinary passenger. Some of them, indeed, amused themselves by turning the hand round until the register showed that the omnibus had carried an impossible number of people. This amusement was getting very popular when Shillibeer put an end to it by removing the clocks and trusting to his conductors' honour—a confidence which was proved, time after time, to be entirely misplaced.

But, in spite of all obstacles, Shillibeer prospered, and in less than nine months had twelve omnibuses at work. A few of these were two-horse omnibuses carrying twelve passengers inside and two outside. Some ran from Paddington to

SHILLIBEER'S THIRD OMNIBUS.

the Bank, *viâ* Oxford Street and Holborn. On

all these new vehicles "Shillibeer" was painted in large letters on the sides, instead of "Omnibus."

The Post Office authorities were the first to copy Shillibeer's vehicles. They had four built, resembling the originals in every respect save the painting and lettering. On September 23, 1829, these vehicles—accelerators they were called—started at half-past eight in the morning from the back of the General Post Office for the western and north-western districts. Each accelerator carried twelve or thirteen letter-carriers, who were put down at various points to begin their delivery.

A little later, Shillibeer's brother-in-law started some omnibuses which ran along the Caledonian Road, and were known as "Caledonians." These, too, were successful, and many years later became the property of Mr. Wilson, the once famous Islington omnibus proprietor. Wilson's "Favorites" were known to every Londoner, and the "Caledonians" were merged into them. At the present day the "Favorites" belong to the London General Omnibus Company, Limited, and on their way from the Nag's Head, Holloway, to West Kensington and Fulham traverse their original road.

In 1832, wishing to still further increase the

number of his omnibuses, Shillibeer took into partnership Mr. William Morton, a Southwell publican, who sold his business to join him. The partnership was dissolved in January, 1834, Morton taking as his share of the business the whole of the New Road omnibuses. He failed, however, to make them pay, and sold them at a great loss. Eventually he became so reduced in circumstances that he applied for, and obtained, a position as an omnibus conductor, but was discharged for drunkenness, and, in a fit of despondency, committed suicide at his lodgings in Little Carlisle Street, Edgware Road. At the inquest, Shillibeer's enemies—of whom he had a large number among short-stage-coach proprietors—endeavoured to prove that the deceased had been swindled over his omnibus partnership. But these charges were shown to be the outcome of jealousy and petty spite, and it was proved that, in giving over the New Road omnibuses to his late partner, Shillibeer had behaved with great generosity, for that was the only line on which there was no opposition. The omnibuses were paying excellently at the time of the dissolution of partnership, but Morton mismanaged them. The person to whom he sold them soon made them as remunerative as they had been under Shillibeer's management. In fact, the New Road route was the best patronised, and, in 1837, there were fifty-four omnibuses on that road. The fares were then sixpence any distance.

In the same year that Shillibeer took Morton into partnership, there were several lines of omnibuses running in opposition to him, for the old short-stage-coach proprietors were now alive to the fact that there was much money to be made out of omnibuses; but the original vehicles had the reputation of being excellently conducted, and, consequently, were preferred by the public. Aware of this, the proprietors of some opposition omnibuses had the impudence to paint on the panels of their vehicles the word "Shillibeer." Shillibeer then named his omnibuses "Shillibeer's Original Omnibuses."

Some of the opposition proprietors, however, were men of sufficient enterprise to object to remaining mere imitators of Shillibeer, and tried their hardest to make their omnibuses more attractive than those of their great rival. One man made all his coachmen wear a wooden ring on each arm with strings attached to them which ran along each side of the roof of the omnibus and out at the back to the conductor. The passenger would then pull the cord or tell the conductor which side he wished to be put down, and if it were the near side the left string would be pulled; but if the passenger desired to get out on the off side the conductor would pull the right string, and the coachman would drive across the road and come to a standstill on what is now the wrong side of the road. It seems strange that such a proceeding should have been allowed in London, but the arrangement was very popular with passengers, who grumbled and wrote letters to the proprietors if the strings were absent or defective. Very soon after the introduction of such strings there were few omnibuses in London without them, and they remained in fashion for many years.

Many omnibuses had clocks fixed in them for the convenience of passengers, and to ensure conductor and coachman keeping their time. Bells did not come into use until many years later. When a conductor wanted his coachman to stop he usually shouted to him. When he wished him to go on he shouted again or banged the door.

Mr. Cloud, who ran omnibuses from the White

Horse, Haymarket, to Chelsea and Hammersmith —fares one shilling and half a crown—eclipsed Shillibeer in one respect. Shillibeer supplied his patrons with newspapers and magazines; Cloud provided his with books by well-known authors. A little bookcase, well filled, was fixed in each of his omnibuses at the end near the horses. Books were expensive in those days, and many people rode to Hammersmith and back for the sole purpose of reading a particular one which they knew to be in the omnibus library. But this admirable innovation was abused shamefully by the passengers, who appeared to consider it no sin to purloin the volumes. Disgusted at the dishonesty of his patrons, Mr. Cloud announced publicly that, in consequence of the thefts, his libraries would be discontinued. The bookcases were removed, and in place of each a seat was fixed, thereby enabling the omnibus to accommodate thirteen inside passengers instead of twelve. Other omnibus proprietors decided that their vehicles should also carry thirteen passengers, but provided no additional accommodation. A conductor would tell a person that there was room inside, but when the passenger entered he would find the six seats on either side occupied. If he happened to be a stout party, the burning question was on which side ought he to sit. The matter was generally settled by the new-comer flopping down on some one's lap. Then a quarrel would ensue. As late as 1882 an omnibus with a seat in front of the fareboard was running from Oxford Circus to Hendon, *viâ* Kilburn. It was a most uncomfortable seat, but, nevertheless, it was nearly always occupied, for the conductor, being a very amusing fellow, had a knack of quickly soothing passengers who protested against sitting on a small, cramped seat.

Soon after the removal of the bookcases, some of the Hammersmith omnibuses acquired the habit of loitering, and thereby obstructing the streets. By Act of Parliament, the police had the power to take into custody the driver of any public vehicle who obstructed the high road and refused to move on. One morning they exercised their power by pulling two omnibus-drivers from their boxes and taking them to the police-station. The following day the drivers were fined forty shillings or a month's imprisonment. For a few days there was no loitering on the Hammersmith Road. But one Saturday evening an omnibus pulled up at Knightsbridge in such a position as to obstruct the traffic. A policeman shouted fiercely to the driver to move on, but the coachman calmly shook his head and would not budge an inch. Two policemen promptly rushed forward to pull him from his seat and take him into custody, but, to their astonishment, found that he was chained to the box and the chain fastened by a huge padlock. Their attempts to remove him were useless. Then several other omnibuses came along, and pulled up close to the first one. The drivers of these were also chained to their boxes, and amused themselves and the crowd by chaffing the police and shaking their chains at them. After remaining at Knightsbridge for some considerable time, they drove away in triumph, only, however, to be fined a few days later.

About this time shopkeepers began to complain that omnibuses prevented their customers driving up to their doors in their carriages, and Mr. Shufflebotham, a silk mercer of Ludgate Hill, championing their cause, applied for summonses against twenty-four conductors for loitering. Under an old Act of Parliament, any stage-coach driver taking up or setting down passengers in the streets was liable to a penalty of not less than £5. All the conductors were fined, but public opinion was by no means favourable to the shopkeepers, and further attempts to prove that private carriages had a greater right to the public streets than omnibuses failed completely. On one occasion an alderman had before him a hundred and twenty conductors charged with the fearful offence—in tradesmen's eyes—of stopping their omnibuses a few moments in front of a shop when a carriage was waiting to pull up there. The alderman discharged every one of the defendants, and his action was so popular that, until a year or two ago, no one had the impudence to suggest that the days of class legislation should be restored—that omnibuses which carry twenty-six passengers should be turned out of the main streets to make room for private carriages with their burden of four.

On January 7, 1832, a new Stage-Coach Act came into force. It had been passed specially to permit omnibuses and short-stage-coaches to take up and set down passengers in the streets.

## CHAPTER III

Shillibeer runs omnibuses in opposition to a railway—Extraordinary action of the Stamp and Taxes Office—Shillibeer is ruined—He appeals to the Government for compensation—Government promises not fulfilled—Shillibeer becomes an undertaker.

SHORTLY after dissolving partnership with Morton, Shillibeer relinquished his metropolitan business and began to run omnibuses from London to Greenwich and Woolwich, placing twenty vehicles on the road. It was a very bold step, considering that a railway from London to Greenwich had been decided upon; but there were many people who believed that the railway was doomed by his action. In fact, the following song, entitled "Shillibeer's Original Omnibus *versus* the Greenwich Railroad," which expressed that opinion, was sold extensively in the streets.

"By a Joint-Stock Company taken in hand,
A railroad from London to Greenwich is plann'd,
But they're sure to be beat, 'tis most certainly clear,
Their rival has got the start—George Shillibeer.

"I will not for certainty vouch for the fact,
But believe that he means to run over the Act
Which Parliament pass'd at the end of last year,
Now made null and void by the new Shillibeer.

"His elegant omnis, which now throng the road,
Up and down every hour most constantly load;
Across all the three bridges how gaily appear,
The *Original Omnibus*—George Shillibeer.

"These pleasure and comfort with safety combine,
They will neither blow up nor explode like a mine;
Those who ride on the rail-road might half die with fear—
You can come to no harm in the safe Shillibeer.

"How exceedingly elegant fitted, inside,
With mahogany polished—soft cushions—beside
Bright brass ventilators at each end appear,
The latest improvements in the new Shillibeer.

"Here no draughts of air cause a crick in the neck,
Or huge bursting boiler blows all to a wreck,
But as safe as at home you from all danger steer,
While you travel abroad in the gay Shillibeer.

"Then of the exterior I safely may say
There never was yet any carriage more gay,
While the round-tire wheels make it plainly appear
That there's none run so light as the smart Shillibeer.

"His conductors are famous for being polite,
Obliging and civil, they always act right,
For if just complaint only comes to his ear,
They are not long conductors for George Shillibeer.

"It was meant that they all should wear dresses alike,
But bad luck has prompted the tailors to strike.
When they go to their work, his men will appear
*À la Française, Conducteur à Mons. Shillibeer.*

"Unlike the conductors by tailors opprest,
His horses have all in new harness been drest:
The cattle are good, the men's orders are clear,
Not to gallop or race—so says Shillibeer.

"That the beauties of Greenwich and Deptford may ride
In his elegant omni is the height of his pride—
So the plan for a railroad must soon disappear
While the public approve of the new Shillibeer."

But, unfortunately for Shillibeer, the plan for the Greenwich railway did not disappear. It was carried out, and when, in 1835, the railway was opened, the earnings of Shillibeer's omnibuses began to decrease ominously. For a time Shillibeer struggled on manfully, but the fight with the railway was an expensive one, and getting into arrears with his payments to the Stamp and Taxes Office, his omnibuses were seized and not permitted to be worked until the money was paid. This unreasonable action on the part of the Stamp Office was repeated three or four times, and the heavy expenses and hindrance to business caused thereby brought about Shillibeer's failure.

Acting on the advice of his many sympathisers, Shillibeer appealed, in 1838, to the Lords of the Treasury for compensation for the injustice done to him, with the result that, shortly after, he was offered the position of Assistant Registrar of

Licences, created by the Bill just passed for the better regulation of omnibuses in and near the Metropolis. This Act, the second one dealing with omnibuses, made it compulsory that the words "Metropolitan Stage Carriage," the Stamp Office number, and the number of passengers that each vehicle was licensed to carry should be painted, in a conspicuous manner, both on the inside and outside of every omnibus. Drivers and conductors were compelled to wear numbered badges, so as to afford means of identification in case of misconduct. Licences were not to be transferred or lent under a penalty of £5, and the omnibus proprietors were forbidden, under a penalty of £10, to allow any unlicensed person to act as driver or conductor, except in the case of sudden illness of the licensed man.

Shillibeer had been led to believe that he would receive the appointment of Registrar of Licences, and was, therefore, greatly disappointed when the Assistant Registrarship was offered him. He declined it, and renewed his applications to the Lords of the Treasury for compensation for the loss he had suffered through the almost criminal stupidity of the Stamp and Taxes Office.

At length their Lordships appointed their Financial Secretary, Mr. Gordon, to inquire into his case, and that gentleman's investigation of the facts proved to their complete satisfaction that Shillibeer had been cruelly wronged by the Stamp and Taxes Office. Thereupon, they promised Shillibeer that he should receive a Government appointment, or a sum of money, that would compensate him for the loss he had suffered. Mr. Gordon was then instructed to apply to the Marquis of Normanby and the Right Hon. Henry Labouchere, the heads of two Government departments, to appoint Shillibeer Inspector-General of Public Carriages, or to give him an appointment on the Railway Department at the Board of Trade. Unfortunately both of these applications were unsuccessful. Mr. Gordon then applied for and obtained for Shillibeer the promise of one of the twenty-five appointments of Receiver-General of County Courts, which were just then being established. But once again Shillibeer was doomed to disappointment. Mr. Gordon resigned his position of Secretary to the Lords of the Treasury, but, before ceasing his duties, he told Shillibeer that, if the Miscellaneous Estimates for the year had not been made up, his name would have been placed in them for a grant of £5000. Moreover, he promised to impress upon his successor the necessity of seeing that Shillibeer received his appointment and grant. He received neither. His claims were not disputed, but unjustly ignored.

At last Shillibeer came to the conclusion that it was useless to place reliance in Government promises. He, therefore, started business as an undertaker, in premises adjoining Bunhill Fields Burial-ground, and the following advertisement appeared continually in the daily papers and elsewhere :—

"*Aux Étrangers. Pompes.*

"Funèbres sur le systeme de la Compagnie Générale des Inhumations et Pompes Funèbres à Paris. Shillibeer's, City Road, near Finsbury Square, où l'on parle Français. Every description of funerals, from the most costly to the most humble, performed much lower than any other funeral establishment. Catholic fittings from Paris. Gentlemen's funerals from 10 guineas. Tradesmen's and artisans', £8, £6, and £4."

In a few years Shillibeer was well known as an

undertaker, and gave evidence before the Board of Health on the subject of the scheme for extra-mural sepulture. But his success as an undertaker, which must have been very gratifying to him after losing many thousands of pounds as an omnibus proprietor, robbed him of posthumous fame by preventing his name becoming as much a household word as is Hansom's. For several years after his pecuniary interest in omnibuses had ceased the vehicles which he had introduced into England were called "Shillibeers" more frequently than "Omnibuses," but as soon as his "Shillibeer Funeral Coaches" became well advertised, people did not like to say that they were going for a ride in a Shillibeer, in case they might be misunderstood. So the word "Shillibeer," which would in time have superseded "Omnibus," and been spelt with a small "s," was discarded, and is now almost forgotten.

Shillibeer was also associated with Mr. G. A. Thrupp, the author of "The History of the Art of Coachbuilding," Mr. John Peters, Mr. Robson, and Mr. Lewis Leslie in efforts to obtain a reduction of the heavy taxes on carriages. Mr. Thrupp has described Shillibeer to me as a big, energetic man, with a florid complexion, and brisk both in his movements and his speech.

Shillibeer died at Brighton on August 22, 1866, aged sixty-nine, and it is not to our credit that we have done nothing to perpetuate the memory of one to whom we owe as delightful a form of cheap riding as could be desired.

# CHAPTER IV

Introduction of steam omnibuses—The "Autopsy," the "Era," and the "Automaton"—Steam omnibuses a failure.

SOME years before Shillibeer introduced omnibuses into England, a number of experienced engineers had devoted themselves to the invention of steam carriages, and so satisfied were they with their achievements that they felt justified in predicting that horse-drawn vehicles were doomed. Once more, however, we see the truth of the saying that threatened institutions live long, for the elimination of the horse is still an event of the distant future. Sir Charles Dance, Dr. Church, Colonel Maceroni, Messrs. Frazer, Goldsworthy Gurney, Hancock, Heaton, Maudsley, Ogle, Redmond, John Scott Russell, Squire, and Summers were the leading men interested in the building of steam carriages, but few of them produced vehicles which are deserving of being remembered. Mr. (afterwards Sir) Goldsworthy Gurney was the first to invent

GURNEY'S STEAM CARRIAGE.

a steam carriage that ran with anything like success. His "Improved Steam Carriage"—an ordinary barouche drawn by an engine instead of horses—accomplished some very creditable journeys, including a run from London to Bath and back at the rate of fifteen miles an hour.

The first real steam omnibuses, the "Era" and "Autopsy," were invented by Walter Hancock, of Stratford, and placed on the London roads in 1833. Hancock had invented steam carriages before Shillibeer's omnibuses were introduced, but the "Autopsy" and the "Era" were the first which he constructed with the idea of entering into competition with the popular horse-drawn vehicles. The "Era" was the better omnibus of the two, and the most flattering things were said and predicted of it. Enthusiasts declared that omnibuses of the "Era" type would enable passengers to be carried at a cheaper rate and greater speed than by Shillibeer's vehicles.

The "Era" ran from Paddington to the Bank, the same route as the horse-drawn omnibuses, and carried fourteen passengers, the fare being sixpence all the way. It travelled at the rate of ten miles an hour, and consumed from 8 to 12 lbs. of coke, and 100 lbs. of water per mile. But, in spite of what the enthusiasts of the day wrote, the "Era" was by no means a success, for it broke down continually, and frequently a considerable time elapsed before it could resume the journey. Our grandfathers, who took life more leisurely than we, did not appear to be greatly annoyed at these

THE "AUTOPSY" STEAM OMNIBUS.

collapses. An hour's delay in reaching their destination was of little consequence to those who could afford to live in the suburbs, and as the steam omnibuses—when they did run—were guided easily and escaped collisions, they were perfectly satisfied, assuring themselves that in a few years, at the most, some means would be found for making the vehicles stop only when required. Moreover, they were a novelty, and as such were patronised for a time. Unfortunately for Hancock, the eccentricities of the "Autopsy" and "Era" increased as the months went on, although the two vehicles continued to run after all the steam omnibuses by other makers had been taken off the roads. Nevertheless, Hancock was not dispirited, and in July, 1835, started his last, and best, steam

THE "ERA" STEAM OMNIBUS.

omnibus—the "Automaton." This was a larger vehicle than his previous ones, being built to carry twenty-two passengers, and to travel at an average speed of thirteen miles an hour. On its trial trip to Romford and back, it did not, however, succeed in attaining a better average than eleven miles an hour. Certainly faster travelling was not desirable in London streets, but on one occasion the "Automaton" was driven at full speed along the Bow Road, and covered a mile at the rate of twenty-one miles an hour. And that record run was the more remarkable as, when it was made, the omnibus carried twenty passengers.

Mr. Hancock was delighted with the working of the "Automaton," and, on the strength of its performance, forgot all his previous failures and wrote light-heartedly: "Years of practice have now put all doubts of the economy, safety, and superiority of steam travelling on common roads at rest, when compared with horse travelling; and I have now in preparation calculations founded upon actual practice, which, when published, will prove that steam locomotion on common roads is not unworthy the attention of the capitalist, though the reverse has been disseminated rather widely of late by parties who do not desire that this branch of improvement should prosper against the interests of themselves."

The "parties" referred to were the London horse-drawn omnibus proprietors, who, according to the steam omnibus owners, indulged in various tricks for making their rivals' vehicles come to grief. Their chief offence was said to be covering the roads with loose stones some inches deep, a proceeding well calculated to injure the steam omnibuses. Unfortunately for the steam omnibus people's story, there is no explanation given of how it was that their rivals were permitted to interfere with the public roads. But how the rumour arose is easily explained. The inventors of steam carriages had proclaimed loudly that their vehicles would not wear out the road as quickly as ordinary carriages, for they had wide tyres and, of course, no horses' hoofs. But, before long, the local authorities came to the conclusion that the reverse was the case—that the steam carriages damaged the roads much more quickly than horse-drawn ones did—and grew anxious to put a stop to the increase of such vehicles. Gloucester had shown them in 1831 how that could be done. A steam carriage ran between Gloucester and Cheltenham twice a day for three months, but when the local authorities discovered that it was cutting up the roads, they came to the conclusion that strong measures would have to be adopted to put an end to the nuisance. So they strewed with loose stones nearly two feet deep the road which the horseless vehicle traversed, and in trying to pass over this obstruction the steam carriage was disabled.

Other towns in England and Scotland hastened to follow the example of Gloucester, and in a few months the number of steam carriages in Great Britain was reduced considerably. Then Parliament passed a sheaf of local Turnpike Bills, imposing exceedingly heavy tolls upon steam carriages, with the result that soon all such vehicles had ceased to run in the provinces.

But no such thing as strewing the roads with loose stones was ever adopted in London, and Hancock's omnibuses had as fair a trial as any reasonable being could desire. The "Automaton," the best steam omnibus ever built, was, unmistakably a failure, although Hancock, by publishing some statistics of its first five months at work, gave people the impression that it was a great success. In the 712 journeys which it made it carried 12,761 passengers — not a remarkable number, considering that it ran under favourable circumstances. That is to say, that when it was found that the interest in the "Automaton" was waning on one route, it was put immediately to another. The majority of journeys were from the City to Islington and back, but on some days the omnibus ran to Paddington, and on others to Stratford. One morning, on its way to the Bank, it came into collision with a waggon at Aldgate, and Hancock, in his report of

THE "AUTOMATON" STEAM OMNIBUS.

its performances, declared that to be the only accident worth mentioning. Apparently occasional break-downs did not count.

But the public's patronage of the "Automaton" grew less as time went on. People soon found that riding in horse omnibuses was far more enjoyable. Moreover, they discovered that they were much more reliable, the falling of a horse and a minute or two's delay caused thereby, being the worst that ever happened to them. The "Automaton," however, could not even be relied upon to start when desired.

In spite of loss of patronage, the "Automaton" dragged on its existence until 1840, when the Turnpike Acts were enforced in London, and gave Hancock the opportunity of discontinuing his steam omnibus and posing as an ill-used man.

And so came to an end the first attempt to run horseless omnibuses in London.

# CHAPTER V

Some old omnibus names—Story of the "Royal Blues"—Omnibus racing—Complaints against conductors—Passengers' behaviour—The well-conducted conductor—The ill-conducted conductor—The "Equirotal Omnibus."

WHILE Hancock's steam omnibuses were endeavouring to win public support, horse omnibuses were in a very flourishing condition, and their proprietors were opening new lines in all the chief parts of London.

In 1837 there were fourteen omnibuses running from Blackheath to Charing Cross; twenty-seven from Chelsea to Mile End Gate; forty-one from Piccadilly to Blackwall; nineteen from Hampstead to Holborn, Charing Cross, and the Bank; seventeen from the Angel, Islington, to the Elephant and Castle; and twenty-five from Edgware Road (the spot where Sutherland Avenue now joins Maida Vale) to the Bank. There were also many omnibuses running into the City from Putney,

Kew, Richmond, Deptford, Greenwich, Lewisham, Holloway, Highbury, Hornsey, Highgate, Hackney, Homerton, Clapton, Enfield, Edmonton, Peckham, Brixton, Norwood, Kennington, Dulwich, Streatham, and elsewhere.

At that time it was the fashion to give each omnibus line a distinctive name, and people soon understood that a "Favorite" went to Islington, an "Eagle" to Pimlico, and so on. The chief lines were the "Favorites," the "Eagles," the "Wellingtons," the "King Williams," the "Napoleons," the "Victorias," the "Nelsons," the "Marlboroughs," the "Hopes," "Les Dames Blanches," the "Citizens," the "Emperors," the "Venuses," and the "Marquess of Westminsters." At the present day the "Atlases," the "Favorites," the "Paragons," the "Royal Blues," and the "Times," are the only omnibuses which have names.

The "Eagles" were green omnibuses, and ran from the "Compasses," at Pimlico, to Blackwall, *viâ* Piccadilly. They belonged to a Mr. John Clark, and old 'busmen declare that one day, as an "Eagle" was passing Hyde Park Corner, Her Majesty Queen Victoria, then unmarried, overtook it, and by some means or other her long habit was caught by the handle of the open door. Clark, who, so the story runs, was acting as conductor on that occasion, released it instantly, and Her Majesty graciously thanked him for his promptitude. In commemoration of this incident, Clark had the omnibus painted blue, and substituted for the word "Eagle" on the panels, the words "Royal Blue." Moreover, he had a picture of Her Majesty on horseback painted on the panel of the door After a time he called all his omnibuses on that line "Royal Blues," but the original "Royal Blue" was the only one that bore a picture of the Queen.

But the first half of the above story is not correct. What really happened is as follows:—Clark was driving one of his omnibuses by Hyde Park Corner, when suddenly Her Majesty approached on horseback. He endeavoured to pull out of the way, but, as the road was partially blocked, it was not an easy thing to do. However, being an excellent whip, he succeeded, and the Queen, who had witnessed his efforts, most graciously bowed to him as she rode by.

For many years the picture of the Queen painted on the Royal Blue omnibus was one of the sights pointed out to visitors to London. Eventually, wishing to preserve the picture, Clark had it cut out of the omnibus door and framed, and it is now in the possession of his daughter.

The "Royal Blues," which were among the first omnibuses sold to the London General Omnibus Company, now run from Victoria to King's Cross *viâ* Piccadilly and Bond Street.

The "Favorites" were named after a Parisian line of omnibuses called *Les Favorites*. The drivers and conductors wore dark blue suits with brass buttons. These omnibuses had, as at present, the word "Favorite" painted in large letters along the panels, and an opposition proprietor imitated them as closely as he dared by having "Favor me" painted on the sides of his omnibus. But the most formidable rivals of the "Favorites" were the "Hopes," and the racing between these omnibuses became decidedly exciting. A "Favorite" and a "Hope" would start together from the corner opposite the Angel, and race madly down the City Road to the Bank. But the accidents which they caused in their wild career became so appallingly numerous that the Islington Vestry offered a reward to any one giving such information as would lead to the conviction of any driver. This action certainly checked the racing proclivities of the Islington omnibus drivers, but in other parts of London racing flourished for many years. Down the Haymarket from Coventry Street was a favourite racing-ground. Then, as now, there was a cab-rank in the centre of the road, and two omnibuses would race down, one each side of it, and frequently come into collision with each other at the end. Many passengers encouraged the coachmen to race, and when accidents occurred to the horses or omnibuses, frequently subscribed to pay for the damage.

Some of the omnibus proprietors possessed very inferior stock, and the horses to be seen pulling their vehicles were a disgrace to London. A story is told of a coachman out of work who applied to one of these proprietors for a job.

"Ever driven a 'bus before?" the proprietor asked.

"Yes, sir. I drove a Kingsland 'bus."

"H'm. Discharged, I suppose."

"No, sir. I left because I wanted a change."

"How many accidents have you had?"

"None at all, sir."

"Smart coachman! Have you let many horses down?"

"Never let one down, sir."

"Get out of my yard," shouted the proprietor, fiercely; "you're no good to me. I want a man who's had plenty of practice at getting horses up. Mine are always falling down."

About this time, the latter part of the thirties, omnibus conductors began to fall into disrepute. The chief complaints against them, apart from their ordinary rudeness to passengers, were that when they were wanted to stop the omnibus they were always busy talking to the coachman along the roof, and that they banged the doors too violently whenever a person entered or got out. Others complained of their shouting unnecessarily, and of standing at the door gazing in at the passengers, thereby preventing fresh air from coming in, and polluting the atmosphere with their foul breath. Moreover, the "cads," as the conductors were now called, were not at all careful to keep objectionable people out of their omnibuses, and one passenger, an old lady, had an exciting experience. She entered an omnibus, and the door was banged behind her in the usual nerve-shattering way. "Right away, Bill!" the conductor shouted, and before the poor old lady had recovered from the shock of the door slamming, the omnibus started, and she was pitched into the far dark corner, and fell against some men sitting there, who answered her timid apologies with an outburst of the vilest language imaginable. The old lady, horrified at their abuse, began to rebuke them, but stopped short, terrified, when she discovered that her fellow-passengers were three villainous-looking convicts, chained together and in charge of a warder. She screamed to the conductor to stop the omnibus, but the conductor was, as usual, talking to the driver, and did not heed her cries. Then she opened the door to get out, and, in her excitement, fell into the road. The conductor jumped down, picked her up, demanded the fare, and got it. "Right away, Bill!" he shouted, and the omnibus drove on, leaving the old lady, bruised and trembling, in the middle of the road.

While many people were complaining of the omnibus conductors' behaviour, a large number of regular riders declared that it was but little worse than that of many passengers, and in January,

1836, the *Times* published the following guide to behaviour in omnibuses :—

OMNIBUS LAW.

1. Keep your feet off the seats.
2. Do not get into a snug corner yourself, and then open the windows to admit a north-wester upon the neck of your neighbour.
3. Have your money ready when you desire to alight. If your time is not valuable, that of others may be.
4. Do not impose on the conductor the necessity of finding you change ; he is not a banker.
5. Sit with your limbs straight, and do not let your legs describe an angle of forty-five, thereby occupying the room of two persons.
6. Do not spit upon the straw. You are not in a hog-sty, but in an omnibus, travelling in a country which boasts of its refinement.
7. Behave respectfully to females, and put not an unprotected lass to the blush because she cannot escape from your brutality.
8. If you bring a dog, let him be small and confined by a string.
9. Do not introduce large parcels ; an omnibus is not a van.
10. Reserve bickerings and disputes for the open field. The sound of your own voice may

be music to your own ears—not so, perhaps, to those of your companions.

11. If you will broach politics or religion, speak with moderation; all have an equal right to their opinions, and all have an equal right not to have them wantonly shocked.
12. Refrain from affectation and conceited airs. Remember you are riding a distance for sixpence which, if made in a hackney-coach, would cost you as many shillings; and that should your pride elevate you above plebeian accommodations, your purse should enable you to command aristocratic indulgences.

Excellent advice, undoubtedly, and some of it might be taken to heart, with good results, by hundreds of omnibus passengers of to-day.

As time passed, the behaviour of the conductors grew worse. This was due chiefly to the indifference of the omnibus proprietors. If their conductors paid in a certain amount daily, they were quite satisfied with them, and by no means thankful to passengers who complained of their misbehaviour. The omnibus proprietor of this period was a much lower class of man than George Shillibeer. In most cases he himself had been a driver or conductor, and, on becoming an employer, his chief anxiety was to prevent his men growing rich at his expense. Knowing from experience what an omnibus could earn in various seasons and weather, he took every precaution possible to guard against his men retaining as large a portion of the earnings as he himself had pocketed when a conductor. The men who paid daily the sum he demanded were the conductors he preferred, and these usually were the passenger-swindling, bullying specimens, and thoroughly deserved their name—" cads."

In January, 1841, the *Times* printed the following description of two classes of conductors:—

### The Well-conducted Conductor

1. Never bawls out " Bank—Bank—City—Bank ! " because he knows that passengers are always as much on the look-out for him as he is for them, so that these loud and hideous shouts are quite unnecessary.
2. Never bangs the omnibus door after he has let a passenger in or out, but makes it a rule to shut it as quietly as possible.
3. Always takes care that there are two check strings or straps running along the roof of the omnibus, on the inside, and communicating with the arms of the driver by two

large wooden or other rings which are easily slipped on and off.

4. Is careful also to have a direction conspicuously placed inside the omnibus, announcing to the passengers that if they wish to be set down on the right hand they will pull the right-hand check-string or strap, and if they wish to be set down on the left hand they will pull the left-hand check-string. By this arrangement the passenger is set down exactly where he wishes to be, and all the bawling is prevented.
5. Never stands at the omnibus door staring in upon the passengers, but sits down upon the seat provided for him outside. In this way he knows that he gains a double advantage: he is saved the fatigue of standing during a whole journey, and by looking backwards as the driver looks forwards, persons who wish to ride are more easily seen than if the driver and conductor are both looking the same way.
6. Never allows the driver to go on till the passengers are safely seated, and always directs him to pull up close either to the right or left hand of the street or road.

### The Ill-conducted Conductor

1. Always bawls out "Bank—Bank—City—Bank—Bank—Bank—City—City—Bank—Bank—Bank!" by which disgusting noise his own lungs are injured, the public peace is disturbed, and not any advantage gained.
2. Always bangs the door so violently that if you are sitting next the door you are likely to be deafened for life.
3. Never provides any check-string, but compels the passengers who want to be set down to use their sticks, canes, and umbrellas, and loud shouts into the bargain, thereby creating a most intolerable nuisance.
4. Always takes up and sets down his passengers in the middle of the street; by which rudeness they are sometimes bespattered with mud and always exposed to danger.
5. Always stands at the door of the omnibus staring in upon the passengers, particularly after he has been eating his dinner of beef-steak, strong onions, and stale beer; and generally has some cad or other crony standing and talking with him. The air that would otherwise circulate through the omnibus, in the way of ventilation, is obstructed and poisoned.

6. Always bawls out "All right!" before the passengers have taken their seats, by which gross carelessness great inconvenience and even danger are often occasioned.

But it was not only of the drivers and conductors that the public complained. The officials at the inquiry offices stationed at the starting-point of each line, were denounced as being utterly unfitted for the positions they occupied. All were rude, and most of them possessed but little intelligence. One afternoon, about twenty minutes past four, a gentleman entered the omnibus office at the George and Blue Boar, Holborn, and inquired of the clerk whether omnibuses started from there to a certain railway-station.

"Yes," was the reply.

"At what hours?"

"One hour before each train."

"Then I'm just in time to catch the 5.30 one."

"It's all down in writing on that there board."

The traveller turned to the board, and, finding the 5.30 train entered upon it, went out into the street to await the arrival of the omnibus. But after pacing up and down for a quarter of an hour, and seeing no sign of a conveyance, he returned to the office and enquired when it would arrive.

"It's gone," the official said.

"Then it didn't start from here," the traveller declared. "I've been waiting outside since twenty past four."

"What train do you want to catch?"

"The half-past five, to be sure. I told you so."

"Oh, we ain't got no omnibus to catch that train."

"But, man, you said that you had one to each train."

"I told you it was all down in writing on that there board, and you ought to have seen for yourself there ain't no omnibus for the half-past five."

The traveller again turned to the board, and after glancing at it, declared angrily, "There's nothing of the kind stated here!"

The official pointed to a small cross against the 5.30 train, and said triumphantly, "This here mark means there ain't no omnibus."

"Well, how was I to know that?"

"Most gentlemen, when they sees it, asks me what the deuce it means, and I tells them."

"But what do the others do?"

The clerk did not condescend to answer, but took out his pocket-knife and busied himself in peeling an apple.

While the public was busily denouncing the behaviour of 'busmen, a quaint vehicle, named the "equirotal omnibus," was placed on the streets. The inventor, Mr. W. B. Adams, maintained that all vehicles should have four large wheels, instead of two large and two small, and his omnibus was constructed on that principle. It was built in two parts, which were joined together in the middle by a flexible leather passage, to enable it to turn easily. "It will turn with facility in the narrowest streets, without impeding the passage along the interior," Mr. Adams declared, "as the flexible sides move in a circle. With this omnibus two horses will do the work of three; there will be great facility of access and egress; perfect command over the horses; increased ease to the passengers; greater head-room and more perfect ventilation; greater general durability and absence of the usual rattling noise, accompanied by entire safety against overturning."

In spite of Mr. Adams's recommendation, the "equirotal omnibus" did not become popular, and had but a short career.

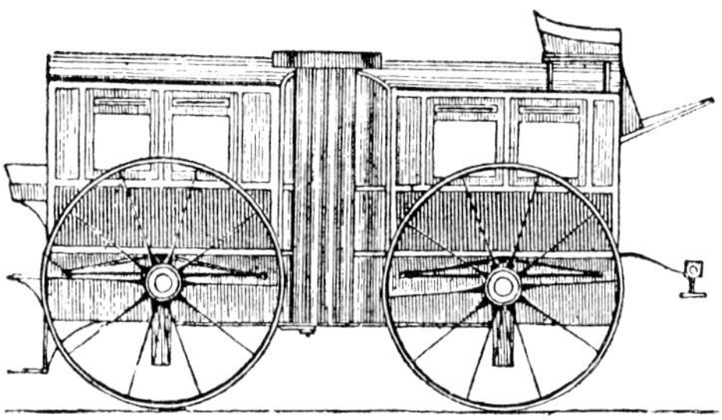

ADAMS'S EQUIROTAL OMNIBUS.

# CHAPTER VI

Twopenny fares introduced—The first omnibus with advertisements—Penny fares tried—Omnibus improvements—Longitudinal seats objected to by the police—Omnibus associations—Newspapers on the "Favorites"—Foreigners in omnibuses—Fat and thin passengers—Thomas Tilling starts the "Times" omnibuses—Mr. Tilling at the Derby—Tilling's gallery of photographs.

On October 21, 1846, a line of omnibuses was started from Paddington to Hungerford Market, Charing Cross, with twopenny fares for short distances. Hitherto the lowest fare had been fourpence. In the same year advertisements appeared for the first time in an omnibus. Mr. Frederick Marriott, of 335, Strand, who started the practice, registered an omnibus, with advertisements displayed on the roof inside, as an article of utility with the title of a "publicity omnibus." Possibly Mr. Marriott—who traded under the name of The Omnibus Publicity Company—reaped little profit from his idea, which was scarcely one that could be protected, but omnibus proprietors are deeply indebted to him, for advertisements are as necessary to them as they are to newspaper and magazine proprietors. Nevertheless, an important newspaper made an amusing slip some years ago about omnibus advertisements. A money-lender advertised in certain omnibuses, and the newspaper in question, becoming aware of the fact, made some very strong remarks concerning the proprietor's conduct in permitting such advertisements to appear. The omnibus proprietor wrote at once to the Editor, pointing out the inconsistency of his paper, which censured him on one page for publishing a money-lender's advertisement, and contained, on another, four advertisements of a similar nature. This letter was not published, and nothing more was said on either side.

Penny fares were introduced in 1849 by some omnibuses running from the Bank to Mile End. For a penny a passenger could ride the whole distance. These omnibuses had but a brief career.

In 1850 several attempts were made to improve the style of omnibuses, with the result that in January, 1851, the knife-board omnibus became general. It was not, however, like the knife-board omnibuses which we still see occasionally, for it carried only nine outside passengers. Two sat on either side of the coachman, and the other five on an uncomfortable seat, about a foot high, running the length of the omnibus. They climbed up at the back on the right-hand side of the door, and sat with their faces to the road. There were no seats on the near side, but occasionally, when passengers were numerous, the conductor would permit men to sit there, with their legs dangling down, over a little rail, in front of the windows. But he always extracted a promise from such passengers that if they smashed the windows they would pay for them. That was a very necessary precaution, as the glass was not of the substantial description now in use.

These new outside seats were very popular with the public, but the police objected to them, on the ground that the climbing up to them was dangerous. The police were undoubtedly in the right, as many accidents testified later, and when they summoned Mrs. Sophia Gaywood for having such seats on the roof of one of her Bayswater omnibuses, they obtained a conviction. But

A KNIFE-BOARD OMNIBUS.

Mrs. Gaywood, like most ladies who have been omnibus proprietors, before and since her time, was rather fond of litigation, and appealed against the conviction. Mr. Wilson of Islington, and other leading omnibus proprietors, gave evidence in her favour, and finally the appeal was allowed and the conviction quashed.

On March 13, 1851, a new patent omnibus was placed on the Bayswater and Charing Cross road. Each passenger had a seat entirely to himself, and every seat was shut off and as secluded as a private box at the theatre. But its career was short. So was that of the London Conveyance Company, which ran omnibuses to the Bank, *viâ* Holborn. This Company's vehicles had the initials L.C.C. painted on them, but not in such large letters as the London County Council have on their omnibuses.

In October of the same year a meeting of London omnibus proprietors was held at the Duke of Wellington, Bathurst Street, Argyle Square, to consider a suggestion made by Mr. Crawford, the originator of the Hungerford and Camden Town Association—now known as the Camden Town Association — for choosing and working new routes at cheap fares. The Hungerford and Camden Town Association, and one or two similar bodies, had come into existence a few years previously through the omnibus proprietors arriving at the conclusion that it would be more remunerative to cease their fierce struggles one with another, and to work harmoniously together. They ran their omnibuses at regular intervals, and the coachmen and conductors were strictly ordered to keep their time. It was an excellent idea, although it afforded little satisfaction to lawyers, many of whom had grown prosperous on the quarrels of omnibus proprietors.

But a reduction in legal expenses was by no means the only saving effected by the amalgamation. Office and management expenses were reduced considerably. The conductors, instead of being engaged by the various proprietors, were now employed and controlled by the secretary of the Association.

At the meeting at the Duke of Wellington new lines were decided upon, the most important one being from Bayswater to the Bank—fourpence all the way, with intermediate twopenny fares. Twenty omnibuses, the majority built by Messrs.

Rock and Gowar, were placed on that road, and were successful from the day of starting. The Associations now in existence are—

Atlas and Waterloo Omnibus Association.
Camden Town ,, ,,
John Bull ,, ,,
King's Cross and Barnsbury Omnibus Association.
King's Cross and Victoria Omnibus Association.
Victoria Station Omnibus Association.
Westminster ,, ,,

Nearly all of the above were in existence before the London General Omnibus Company was started. The Atlas and Waterloo is the largest of the Associations, and its omnibuses run as far south as Gipsy Hill and north as Finchley. Moreover, it claims, and its claim cannot be disputed, to have the prettiest omnibus route in London. That route is from Oxford Circus to Hendon, *viâ* Finchley Road, Child's Hill and Golder's Green.

The chief proprietors having omnibuses in some, or all, of the above Associations are: The London General Omnibus Co., Ltd.; The Star Omnibus Co., London, Ltd.; The Associated Omnibus Co., Ltd.;

The London Omnibus Carriage Co., Ltd.; Thos. Tilling, Ltd.; Birch Bros., Ltd.; and Messrs.

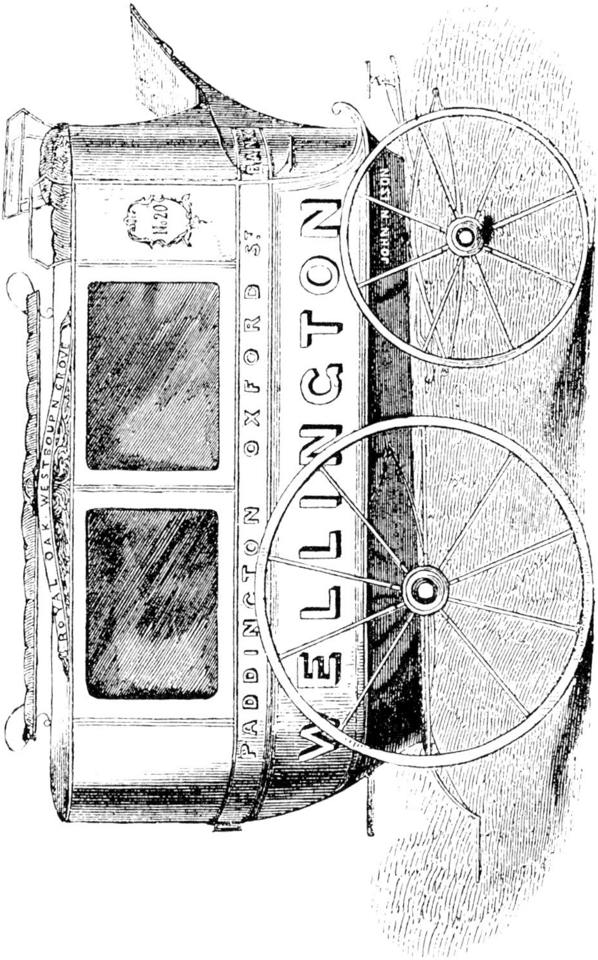


OMNIBUS BUILT BY ROCK AND GOWAR.

Cane, Clinch, French, Glover, and Hearn. The

Associated Omnibus Co., Ltd., was formed last year to acquire and carry on the businesses of The Omnibus Proprietors, Ltd., Mr. John Watkins and Mr. P. Willing Tibbs.

The London Road Car Company, Ltd., and Messrs. Balls Bros. work in friendly opposition to the above Associations.

The "times" in these Associations are very valuable, and when any are placed on the market —which rarely happens—they are snapped up immediately. Until he has bought his "times," no proprietor is recognized in the omnibus business.

In November, 1851, newspapers were placed in the "Favorite" omnibuses for the convenience of passengers. A rack was fixed at the end opposite the door, with a printed notice beneath, asking passengers to replace the papers when done with, and put a penny in the money-box provided for that purpose. It was soon seen that the British public had not changed, in the matter of forgetfulness, since Shillibeer and Cloud's omnibus days. The passengers were continually taking papers away with them, and it was very rarely that the money-box was found to contain anything more valuable than buttons.

In the year of the Great Exhibition, when London was crowded with foreigners, the number of omnibuses was increased considerably; but there were not too many, and proprietors and conductors grew rich in a few months. Many of the conductors fared better than their masters, and when the Exhibition was at an end settled down to some other business with a comfortable sum in hand to give them a good start. Of course, the conductors did not obtain the money in a legitimate manner. The way in which they did obtain it is, however, no secret. Every morning, before starting work, they provided themselves with a quantity of pence, half-pence, and small pieces of silver, for change. Then their chief aim was to fill their omnibuses with foreigners, and give them wrong change when they alighted. If a foreigner gave one of those conductors half a crown for a fourpenny fare, the latter would count out two sixpences and four half-pence, put them in the man's hand, shout out "Right away, Bill!" jump on the step and drive off, leaving the poor fellow puzzling his brain to understand the change. On other occasions the conductor would tell the foreigners that they had reached their destination before they had gone half-way, and the unsuspecting aliens would get out, paying the full fare without a murmur.

Quarrels among the passengers were of everyday occurrence, and the cause of the discord was, almost invariably, the windows. There were usually five windows on each side of the omnibus, which could be opened or closed according to the passenger's fancy. An arrangement better calculated to breed discord could scarcely have been made. The quarrels concerning them were usually somewhat ludicrous—from the fact that the ten windows rattled fearfully, compelling the disputants to yell at each other to make themselves heard. One day a Frenchman and an Italian chanced to be sitting side by side in an omnibus. The Italian pulled up a window just behind them. The Frenchman promptly, and indignantly, lowered it. The Italian excitedly pulled it up again, and this ding-dong performance was continued for some little time, greatly to the amusement of the other passengers. At last, the Frenchman grew desperate, and shattered the glass with his elbow, exclaiming, "Now, Monsieur, you can have ze window up if you likes!"

Many Londoners objected strongly to the overcrowding of omnibuses during the time of the Exhibition, and some, who knew the law, insisted upon having their proper amount of space, no matter who suffered in consequence. The law had declared that every passenger was entitled to sixteen inches of room on the seat; that he might measure it, and any person hindering him from doing so was liable to a penalty of £5. Consequently, many cantankerous people carried yard-measures in their pockets, and insisted upon having their full space. Certainly, sixteen inches is not much room for any man or woman, and a large proportion of the passengers could not possibly squeeze themselves into it; and, because of their inability to do so, quarrels between thin and stout people were of everyday occurrence.

In the year of the Great Exhibition was started the first of Tilling's omnibuses. There have been many English proprietors who have conducted their businesses successfully and honourably, but none came so prominently before the public as George Shillibeer and Thomas Tilling. Both men had interesting careers, but there the similarity ends. Shillibeer, if not a rich man, was very well-to-do when he started his famous omnibuses, and yet he was driven at last into the bankruptcy court, and finished his omnibus career under a financial cloud. Tilling, however, began work without capital, and with but one solitary horse for his stock-in-trade, yet by hard work he achieved success and built up the large business so well known to all Londoners. By 1851, four years after his modest start, he had prospered to an extent which enabled him to put on the road his first omnibus. It was called the "Times," and ran from Peckham to Oxford Circus. At the present day there are some twenty-four "Times" omnibuses on that road. Tilling's "Times" are excellently horsed, and share with the John Bull Association's omnibuses the honour of being the fastest travelling omnibuses in London. Tilling's four-horsed "Times" doing its first morning journey to the West End is the most picturesque omnibus sight in England.

When the first "Times" had proved a success, Mr. Tilling started omnibuses on other roads, and before many years had elapsed there was no name better known to South Londoners than his. At that period it was the morning custom of South

London omnibuses to go round the streets, in the district from which they started, to pick up their regular riders at their houses; but Mr. Tilling would not conform to this practice. He made it

TILLING'S FOUR-HORSE "TIMES."

known that his omnibuses would not collect passengers, but would start from a certain place at a stated time, and people understood that if they wanted to travel by them they would have to go to the starting-place.

Mr. Tilling was by no means an omnibus proprietor only. Before he had been established many years he was the owner of coaches, cabs, wedding carriages, and, in short, carried on the ordinary business of a job master. On Derby Day he had, usually, as many as two hundred horses on the course, and although he was present at Epsom thirty consecutive years, he had always so much to attend to that he never once saw the great race run. In fact, on one occasion, when he got back to Peckham, he surprised his chief clerk, who had been in the office all day, by asking what horse had won. After that it need scarcely be said that Mr. Tilling did not indulge in betting. Indeed, betting and swearing were practices which he would not tolerate among his men, although he was one of the most considerate employers that ever lived. Unspoiled by success, unostentatiously charitable and simple in his tastes, he was held in the highest esteem by every man in his employ, and when he died, in 1893, the loss was felt by each of them to be a personal one.

There exists, at Messrs. Tilling's chief offices, a good-sized room containing a pleasing testimony to the interest which the founder of the firm took in his employees. Mr. Tilling, many years ago, ordered that a photograph should be taken, and hung in that room, of every man who had been in his employ for twenty years. As other men completed their twenty years' service their photographs were taken and added to the collection, and now—for the practice is still maintained—the walls are covered with them.

Many of the men whose photographs adorn the room have been in the Tillings' employ for nearly half a century. One of their "Times" coachmen, whose face is very familiar to frequenters of Regent Street, has driven an omnibus through that thoroughfare for over forty years. His brother has been in the same employ for a still longer period. The office also has its representatives of long service, one gentleman having been engaged there nearly forty years.

Mr. Tilling, as already stated, began business with one horse, but the limited liability company which bears his name has now a stud of over four thousand, and possesses one hundred and sixty omnibuses. The horse with which Mr.

Tilling started business was a grey, and for many years, in fact until he was compelled by his customers' requirements to break the rule, he would purchase no horses that were not of that colour.

# CHAPTER VII

Compagnie Générale des Omnibus de Londres formed—The London General Omnibus Company starts work—Businesses purchased by the Company—It offers a prize of £100 for the best design of an omnibus—The knife-board omnibus introduced—Correspondence system tried—Packets of tickets sold—Yellow wheels—The L.G.O.C. becomes an English Limited Liability Company—The first board of directors—Present position of the Company—The Omnibus: a satire—The Omnibus: a play.

In 1855 the most important event in the history of English omnibuses occurred, for on December 4 of that year a "Société en Commandite" was established in Paris with the title of the "Compagnie Générale des Omnibus de Londres," for the purpose of running omnibuses in London and its suburbs. The directors of this Society, or Company, were sufficiently astute to refrain from making it known to the London public that the enterprise was a French one. They chose an English name for public use, and the earliest notices of their contemplated operations were headed the "London Omnibus Company." Apparently they were unaware that a company of that name had existed and come to a disappointing end, but doubtless this was intimated to them, for the name was changed speedily—before they started work— to the "London General Omnibus Company." Moreover, as the first managers of the company were well-known London omnibus proprietors, there was nothing to make the public suspect that the company was not an English one.

Monday, January 7, 1856, was the day selected by the London General Omnibus Company for taking over and beginning to work the old-established businesses which they had purchased. On that morning Wilson's Islington and Holloway "Favorites" came out of the yards with "London General Onmibus Company" painted on them. The company could not possibly have started work under more auspicious circumstances, for Mr. Wilson was the largest omnibus proprietor in London, and his vehicles, which were known all over the Metropolis, had the reputation of being exceedingly well conducted. The property which Wilson sold to the Company consisted of fifty omnibuses and five hundred horses, and his employees, numbering about one hundred and eighty men, passed into the service of the new Company. On the same day Mr. Leonard Willing and his partners—the former the oldest omnibus proprietor in London—transferred to the Company the Stoke Newington, Kingsland and Dalston lines, consisting of twenty-two omnibuses, two hundred horses, and seventy men.

In a few days several other lines passed into the hands of the Company, making it the owner of one hundred and ninety-eight vehicles and nineteen hundred and forty horses, and the employer of six hundred and seventy men. Of the vehicles purchased seven were four-horse mails, five running to Woodford and two to Barnet. The Company had hoped to start work with five hundred omnibuses, but many of the well-established proprietors could not be persuaded to sell their businesses, and consequently the London General Omnibus Company had to be content, for a time, with three hundred.

The proprietors who did dispose of their businesses, and retired altogether from omnibus proprietorship were: Messrs. Bennet, Breach, Chancellor, Clark, Forge, Fox, Hartley, Hawtrey, Hinckley, Horne, Hunt, Johnson, Kerrison,

Macnamara, Martin, Proome, Roads, Seale, Smith, Webb, Westropp, Williams, Willing, Wilson, and Woodford.

One of the Company's first concerns was to obtain an improved omnibus, and with that end in view the directors offered a prize of £100 for the best plan of one suited to their requirements. There were seventy-four competitors, and the results of their efforts were displayed, in February, 1856, at the Company's office, 454, Strand. The two best plans were sent in respectively by Mr. R. F. Miller and Mr. Wilson, but the judges, Messrs. George Godwin, Joseph Wright, and Charles Manby, were by no means pleased with the work submitted to them, and reported to the directors :—

"We have first to express our regret that although many of the propositions display considerable ingenuity and offer here and there improvements, we do not find any one design of supereminent merit, or calculated in its present shape to afford that increased amount of comfort and accommodation your company, with praiseworthy foresight, desires to give the public, and which, moreover, will doubtless be looked for at your hands.

"Inasmuch, however, as we are required to select one of the designs as the best of those submitted, considered with regard to your stipulations and wants, we beg leave to point out the design No. 64 sent in by Mr. Miller, of Hammersmith. Inquiry of Mr. Miller, and the examination of a full-sized omnibus built by him (after arriving at this determination) have shown us that if his intentions were more completely expressed in his drawing than is the case, the design would be more worthy of the premium.

"We must repeat that we find no design that we can recommend for adoption intact, or which, to speak truly, is worth the premium offered; but there are points about some of them which, being combined, would aid in producing what you and the public desire—a light, commodious, and well-ventilated omnibus.

"GEORGE GODWIN,
"JOSEPH WRIGHT,
"CHARLES MANBY."

Mr. Miller was awarded the prize, but the directors, acting on the advice contained in the judges' report, had their new omnibuses built from a design which combined the best suggestions of several competitors.

In 1857 further improvements were made in the construction of omnibuses, the most important being the placing of five more seats on the roof, thereby making accommodation for fourteen outside passengers. These seats were placed on the near side, and made the "knife-board" omnibus, which has now almost entirely disappeared from London streets, but may be found passing the eventide of its existence in sleepy country towns and populous watering-places.

Before the London General Omnibus Company was a year old it introduced the system of "correspondence," which in Paris had proved profitable to the proprietors and convenient to the public. It was the Company's idea that a passenger might be able to travel from any part of London to another for sixpence. The passenger would get into the omnibus starting from the neighbourhood in which he resided and ride in it until another of the Company's omnibuses, going in the direction he wished to travel, crossed the road, when he would change into it. By that arrangement people were able to ride from Bow to

Hammersmith or from Starch Green to Peckham for sixpence—a tremendous ride for the price, and cheaper than it is at the present day.

The London General Omnibus Company was now increasing rapidly, by purchase and by starting new lines, the number of its omnibuses, and in November, 1857, when the "correspondence" system was at its height, it possessed five hundred and ninety-five on the roads. For these omnibuses, with horses, harness, and good will, the Company paid £400,000—nearly £700 per omnibus. With an increased number of omnibuses the advantages of "corresponding" became greater, and upwards of four thousand people daily showed their appreciation of the system by "corresponding" at the Company's offices opened for that purpose in Oxford Circus, Cheapside, and Bishopsgate. "The system is only in its infancy," the directors declared at that period, and promised that it would be improved greatly. Difficulties, however, arose in the working of the system, which, after a time, was discontinued, never to be tried again.

While the London General Omnibus Company was giving the "correspondence" system a trial, it was making other attempts to win the favour of the public. On the first day of 1857 it began the sale of packets of omnibus tickets, allowing a reduction of ten per cent. on every purchase of £1, and so greatly was this innovation appreciated that on the inauguration day ten thousand tickets were sold at the Company's Strand office alone. Later the sales increased considerably, and many linen-drapers in a large way of business purchased thousands of tickets at a time, and retailed them to their customers at a reduced rate. To ladies whose purchases reached a certain sum they presented tickets free of charge.

Evidently the directors found, after a time, that the practice of selling tickets was not sufficiently remunerative, for it was discontinued. The directors were astute men of business, and while they neglected nothing that would conduce to the efficiency of their service and the comfort of their patrons, they made a number of alterations which reduced to a considerable extent the working expenses of their omnibuses. One of these alterations caused a complete revolution in the colour of omnibus wheels. When the Company started work, omnibus wheels were painted the same colour as the body of the vehicles, and consequently it was necessary to keep a stock of red, blue, green, brown, white, yellow, and chocolate wheels. The directors, however, soon came to the conclusion that if all the wheels were painted one colour it would not be necessary to keep so large a stock in reserve. Therefore they had the wheels of all their omnibuses painted yellow, and the other proprietors, seeing the convenience and saving to be derived from such an arrangement, followed their example, and to-day nearly every omnibus in London, with the exception of those belonging to the railway companies, has yellow wheels.

In the autumn of 1858 it was decided to convert the "Compagnie Générale des Omnibus de Londres" into an English Limited Liability Company, and for that purpose the French Society was dissolved and the London General Omnibus Company, Limited, started to take over its property, good will, existing engagements and liabilities. The latter was registered on November 16, 1858, as a Limited Liability Company, with a nominal capital of £700,000, divided into 175,000 shares of £4 each. The head office of the Company was, of course, in London—454, Strand—but a branch office was opened in Paris, where French shareholders could obtain any information which they required, and where a duplicate transfer-book was kept for the registering of transfers of shares held in France. The number of directors was to be not more than twelve nor less than nine, and at least four of them were to be Frenchmen. The first Board of Directors of the London General Omnibus Company, Limited, was constituted as follows:—

Anthony Nicholas Armani, Esq.
M. Felix Carteret.
Edwin Chadwick, Esq., C.B.
William Halliday Cosway, Esq.
William Stratford Dugdale, Esq.
M. le Comte de Lantivy.
Arthur Macnamara, Esq.
William Sheldon, Esq.
Reginald Thornton, Esq.
M. François Frederic Toché.
M. Antoine Vacossin.
James Willing, Esq.

In his early days Mr. Willing was a man of many businesses. Among other things he was the owner of several toll-gates, the proprietor of many omnibuses, and an advertising contractor. One day he would be found standing at a toll-gate, collecting money from passing vehicles, and the following one he would be seen driving an omnibus. While acting as a 'bus driver he was able to keep a sharp eye on his advertising business, and was frequently annoyed to see that his bills, which were being posted as he drove Citywards, were covered by other people's bills when he returned an hour or two later. To put a stop to that annoyance he started the protected hoardings, which are now so numerous throughout the land.

At the present time there are only two French directors of the London General Omnibus Company, the number of shareholders resident in France having decreased to seven hundred. The office in Paris is still maintained. The number of English shareholders is seventeen hundred.

From the day that the London General Omnibus Company became an English concern, it has enjoyed almost unbroken prosperity. During the half-year ending June 30, 1901, 101,109,572 passengers were carried by its 1373 omnibuses, which ran 15,965,602 miles. The number of horses which it possessed was 16,714. The oats, maize, beans, and peas consumed by the company's horses in six months weighed 25,299 tons.

The Company builds its own omnibuses at its works at Highbury. Its stables are dotted all over London, and some of the newly erected ones are enormous places. Those at Dollis Hill, which accommodate over six hundred horses, are at present surrounded by fields, and so far away from public-houses and other delights of London civilization, that the 'busmen, in disgust, have named it "Klondyke."

From "Klondyke" and many other omnibus stables, a large number of horses have been sent to the seat of war in South Africa. Some time ago the Government made an arrangement with various omnibus companies for the purchase of a certain number of horses in time of war. For each horse the Government pays, in time of peace, 10*s.* per annum. The average price paid for each horse claimed for active service was £60. The horses taken were well seasoned and accustomed to hard work. The sudden requisitioning of many hundreds of their best animals caused the various omnibus companies considerable

RICHMOND CONVEYANCE COMPANY OMNIBUS.

inconvenience. The daily journeys of many of their omnibuses were reduced in number, and coachmen and conductors were consequently unable to earn their usual wages.

Two years after the formation of the London General Omnibus Company there were about 1200 omnibuses in London, only a small proportion of which worked on Sundays. On the majority of roads they ran on week-days at intervals of five minutes, the fares being, in most cases, from twopence to ninepence. Many of the omnibus lines in existence at that time have been altered or curtailed in consequence of railway competition. Among these are the following long-distance routes:—Stratford and Oxford Street, Brentford and St. Paul's, Greenwich and Charing Cross, Richmond, Kew and Bank, Finchley and Bank, Angel and Hampton Court. The Richmond Conveyance Company had some excellent omnibuses, which ran from Richmond to the Bank, *viâ* Mortlake, Barnes, Hammersmith, and Piccadilly. They were built by Mr. H. Gray of Blackfriars.

In the early sixties it began to be recognized that, for men, the best way to see London was from the top of an omnibus. An anonymous poet published, in 1865, a satire on life seen from an

RICHMOND CONVEYANCE COMPANY OMNIBUS. END VIEW.

omnibus roof. It was entitled "The Omnibus." Here are a few lines from it—

> "August four-wheeler! Rolling Paradise!
> Thou Juggernaut to dawdling men and mice!
> Thou blissful refuge to the footsore cit!
> Thou boast of science and inventive wit!
> To thee, in pride careering o'er the stones,
> The homeward labourer drags his weary bones.
> The burdened porter, staggering on the road,
> Climbs up thy hulk and there forgets his load.

For thee the merchant his dull desk forsakes,
And leaves Cornhill to night, and thieves, and rakes.
The lover finds thee pensioner of bliss,—
By thee he speeds to reap the promised kiss.
On thy 'outside,' no muff can plead his qualms,
And us forbid to colour our meerschaums;
Thy ramparts hold we by an ancient lease,
And there unchallenged, smoke the pipe of peace.
All hail! thou kindest gift of human sense!
Thou envy of the wretch—who lacks three-pence!
All hail! thou huge, earth-born leviathan!
Thou rattling, rambling, two-horse caravan!
Thou dry-land ship, breasting in scorn the waves
Of traffic's whirlpool that round Cheapside raves.
Behind thee, competition lies,
And jealousy but breathes a curse and dies.
Poor Francis Train just hissed at thee his spite,
Then, with his 'Tramways' sank in endless night;
And jobbing railways, near thy presence found,
Smitten with shame, hide, fuming 'Under-ground.'
Though trampled curs may curse thee with a bark,
And godless cabmen call thee—'Noah's Ark;'
Majestic vehicle! much slandered friend,
To lowest Tophet we their libels send,
And chaunt thy praises to the City's end.
An eighth world-wonder thine arrival bodes,
Thou greatest, best, Colossus of our roads."

Some years prior to the publication of the above satire, a farcical comedy, entitled "The Omnibus," had been produced at the Theatre Royal, Covent Garden. A man and his wife, seeking rural quietude, take a house in a charming suburb, only to find that omnibuses run to it from London. Nearly every omnibus brings them a load of visitors, who drive the poor man to distraction.

# CHAPTER VIII

The opening of Holborn Viaduct—An omnibus is the first vehicle to cross it—" Viaduct Tommy "—Skid-men.

AFTER a frost or a slight fall of rain, asphalted Victoria Street and Tottenham-court Road, innocent of sand until many poor horses have slipped and fallen and struggled and strained to rise again, are a saddening sight to horse-lovers. But those, and other notorious streets, at their worst never present such a sight as was witnessed daily on Holborn Hill in the first half of the 19th century. It was a cruel, heart-breaking hill for horses to climb, and people who lived on the spot declared that from morning until night, in all weathers, piteous sights were always to be seen. Year after year the cruelty of compelling horses to pull heavily-laden vehicles up the hill was denounced by hundreds of Londoners, and, eventually, the City Corporation put an end to the pitiful sight by building the Holborn Valley Viaduct.

The chief stone was laid by Mr. Thomas Henry Fry, chairman of the Improvement Committee of the Corporation, on June 3, 1867, and on Saturday, November 6, 1869, the Viaduct was opened by Queen Victoria, who came, accompanied by Princess Louise, straight from Blackfriars Bridge, where she had just performed a similar ceremony. In spite of the weather, which threatened at first to be a repetition of the previous day, when London was enveloped in a fog, the crowd was the largest which had ever assembled to greet Her Majesty. On the Viaduct, the tiers of seats erected on either side were filled with a brilliant gathering invited by the Corporation. After the Queen had opened the bridge and departed, and the Corporation's guests had dispersed, the work of clearing away the stands and preparing for the real opening to the public was begun.

Punctually at nine on Monday morning the barrier across the roadway was removed, and at once there was a rush of vehicles whose drivers were eager for the honour of being first across the Viaduct. Thomas Grayson, driving one of the London General Omnibus Company's "City-Atlas" omnibuses, whipped up his horses and won an exciting race amidst the enthusiastic cheers of his passengers. In commemoration of this event, Grayson's regular riders presented him with a new whip, on the handle of which was inscribed the occasion of its presentation. Some of the riders, proud of having been present on the memorable morning, expressed a wish to have a photograph of the omnibus, and Grayson had one taken. In it he is to be seen sitting upright on the box, holding the presentation whip in his hand and driving the pair of horses with which he won the race. Grayson had a large number of copies of this photograph printed, with the following record on the back of each :—

First over the Holborn Viaduct,
On November 8, 1869,
at 9 a.m.
Copies may be had of the Driver,
THOMAS GRAYSON,
1, Victoria Place,
Kilburn.

These photographs Grayson offered for sale at sixpence a copy, and the whole stock was soon purchased by the St. John's Wood people—to whom he was already well known—and his fellow 'busmen. The latter promptly and unanimously dubbed him "Viaduct Tommy," and by that name he was known as long as he lived. No London omnibus driver was ever so well known as "Viaduct Tommy" became, for, as he drove along the streets, quite conscious that he was a public character, other 'bus drivers would say to the passengers

THE FIRST VEHICLE TO CROSS HOLBORN VIADUCT.

sitting beside them, "That's 'Viaduct Tommy,'" and the story of his achievement would follow.

"Viaduct Tommy" continued to drive an omnibus for about a score of years after he became famous, and when, at last, he retired he was not forgotten. The people in the neighbourhood where he resided, during the latter years of his life, took pride in pointing him out to strangers, many of whom, when they heard the story, went up to the old man and had a chat with him about the great event of his life.

Every innovation for the public good ruins a few people who prospered under the old order of things, and the building of Holborn Viaduct was no exception to the rule. A number of men had for years made a living by putting the skids on vehicles before they started down the hill, and one of them, who was largely patronised by omnibus men, earned every day between twelve and fifteen shillings. But when the Viaduct was opened their occupation was gone.

# CHAPTER IX

A new Company—The London and District Omnibus Company—The London Road Car Company, Limited—Its first omnibuses—The garden seats—The flag and its meaning—Foreigners' idea of it—Ticket system—The great strike—The London Co-operative Omnibus Company—Mr. Jenkins and advertisements—The Street Traffic Bill—Outside lamps.

In May, 1878, several influential City men came to the conclusion that there was an opening in London for a new omnibus company, and, believing that the venture would be very profitable, they decided to start one. Remembering, perhaps, where Shillibeer and the London General Omnibus Company received their inspiration, the promoters deputed one of their number to visit Paris, to inspect the omnibuses at work in that city and to take particular notice of the new vehicles being displayed at the Exhibition by the Paris Omnibus Company. After a stay at Paris, this gentleman proceeded to other Continental capitals, and made himself acquainted with the latest improvements in the omnibuses at work in those cities. On his return to London, with a stock of useful ideas, the formation of the new London company was proceeded with at once. The prospectus was drawn up, Memorandum and Articles of Association were prepared, a Board was formed, and everything was proceeding satisfactorily, when quarrels broke out among the proposed Directors. One of them was the owner of a patent omnibus, and proprietorship invested it, in his eyes, with an excellence and superiority over all other omnibuses which his colleagues could not perceive. They refused his request to make this patent omnibus the vehicle of the new company, and that was the cause of the first quarrel. The second, which followed it closely, was also of a personal nature, one man being convinced that he was the best qualified of the Board to become Managing Director, while the others expressed quite a contrary opinion. The result of these quarrels was that the scheme for a new London omnibus company was withdrawn, and not brought forward again until two years had elapsed. Everything went smoothly at the second attempt, and on August 3, 1880, the London and District Omnibus Company, Limited, was incorporated, under the Companies Act, with a capital of £200,000, divided into 20,000 shares of £10 each. On April 7, 1881, the name of the Company was changed to the London Road Car Company, Limited. Six days later the Company began work in a very modest way with three omnibuses, which ran between Hammersmith and Victoria. These omnibuses, all drawn by three horses, were very different from those which the Company now possesses, and in appearance were rather ungainly. The front wheels were very small, and the back ones large. There was no door, or staircase, at the back of the omnibus, and all passengers had to get on the vehicle just behind the coachman. It was found, however, that many accidents occurred to passengers whilst entering and alighting, and, consequently, an alteration was decided upon. The omnibus was turned right about, the back being made the front. The old wheels, which had a crank action, were removed, and ordinary ones substituted. The coachman was promoted to a seat on top of the omnibus, but the door remained unaltered. The steps were considerably improved.

The Company now possesses 455 omnibuses, or

"cars," as it prefers to call them, and a stud of 5206 horses, not including those used in the Jobbing Department.

In the matter of outside accommodation for passengers, the improved omnibuses of the

THE LONDON ROAD CAR COMPANY'S FIRST OMNIBUS.

London Road Car Company were far in advance of those belonging to all other companies and proprietors. In place of the ordinary uncomfortable longitudinal seats, which so frequently led to squabbles between people sitting back to back, the London Road Car Company had the now common and popular garden seats. It was an innovation which met with unqualified approval from the public. To ladies it was a boon which they had never even expected, so accustomed were they to being relegated to the inside of omnibuses. To clamber to the top of the knife-board omnibuses was an impossibility with most of them, and the athletic few who did not find the task an arduous one were rewarded by being considered exceedingly unladylike. In fact, until the London Road Car Company started work, it was an unusual sight to see a female on the top of an omnibus. But now, when the weather is fine, few ladies ride inside if there be room for them on the roof. Truly, the fair sex should be very grateful to the London Road Car Company. Pickpockets, certainly, were deeply indebted to it, for the backs of the garden seats were open, and afforded them special facilities for the exploration of ladies' pockets. After a time this defect was altered.

The popularity of the garden-seat omnibuses did not benefit the London Road Car Company alone, for other companies and proprietors, following its example, built all their new omnibuses with similar seats and staircases. Many of their knife-board omnibuses—too new to be discarded—were converted into the popular style of vehicle. Some of these converted omnibuses were, it must be confessed, a ghastly failure, for, although there was no fault to be found with the staircase, the arrangement on the roof was not only inconvenient, but highly dangerous. The gangway was raised, sometimes almost to a level with the outside rail, and passengers had to be very careful, in stepping down from it to take their seats, that they were not pitched head-first into the road. Fortunately, the worst specimens of these converted omnibuses have long since disappeared from the London streets.

It is surprising that garden-seat omnibuses were not introduced into London long before the Road Car Company was formed, as they had been in use in some Continental cities for thirty years.

At the outset of its career, the London Road Car Company adopted, as a distinctive sign, the diminutive Union Jack which flies at the fore of all its omnibuses. This flag was intended, also, to intimate to the public that the Company was floated with British capital, but, as very few Londoners were aware of the French origin of the

London General Omnibus Company, the hint was not generally understood. Strangely enough, this appeal to the patriotism of Englishmen, has resulted in the Company receiving a large amount of support from foreigners visiting London. They imagine that the Union Jack is a sign that the omnibuses are State-subsidised vehicles, and, to avoid falling into the hands of the dreaded pirates—for the London pirates' notoriety has reached the chief Continental cities—they will ride in no omnibus which does not carry a flag. Sometimes they stand for a long while looking for an omnibus with the Union Jack flying, to discover, eventually, that there are no Road Car omnibuses on that route. One French lady stood at Marble Arch for more than half an hour before a policeman could convince her that no "'bus with a flag" ran to what she called Crick-le-Wood.

The London Road Car Company's flags have on several occasions been utilised for arousing the enthusiasm of London crowds. On Sunday, September 24, 1899, a few unpatriotic Englishmen desecrated the plinth of Nelson's Column by expressing therefrom sympathy with Great Britain's enemies. The reception accorded to them was, naturally, very hostile, and, while the excitement was at its height, a Road Car omnibus passed

A ROAD CAR COMPANY OMNIBUS, 1901.

slowly through the crowd. A passenger, riding on top of the omnibus, no sooner discovered the meaning of the angry shouts, than he pulled the flagstaff from its socket, and waved aloft the little Union Jack. Loud cheers greeted his action, and the pro-Boer orators were taught speedily that Londoners had a healthy objection to their foolish, un-English ravings.

Another innovation of the London Road Car Company was the ticket system, which, although it had been in use on trams for many years, had not, hitherto, been tried on omnibuses. Tickets had certainly been issued on the omnibuses belonging to the Metropolitan Railway, which ran from Portland Road Station to Piccadilly Circus, but it was on a different system entirely. The Metropolitan Railway omnibuses of those days were not like those in use at the present day. They were larger, and the inside was divided into two compartments, the first-class being the portion near the horses. The compartments were separated by a curtain. These omnibuses were patronised chiefly by people residing in the suburbs, tickets being issued at the Metropolitan Railway stations to carry passengers through by train and 'bus to Piccadilly Circus. The conductor collected the railway tickets on the omnibus, and issued other tickets to passengers who had not come by train. These omnibuses were drawn by three horses harnessed abreast. At the present day, almost the only omnibuses drawn by three horses abreast are the red "Favorites"—big, ungainly things,

A METROPOLITAN RAILWAY "UMBRELLA" OMNIBUS, 1901.

which run from Highgate and Islington to the City. They carry nearly fifty passengers, but, in consequence of their size, are not allowed to be in the City after 10 a.m.

The ticket system having worked successfully on the London Road Car Company's omnibuses, the London General Omnibus Company, and the companies and proprietors working in conjunction with it, announced, at the beginning of May, 1891, their intention of adopting it—a decision which created the greatest indignation among their con-

A RED "FAVORITE," 1901.

ductors and coachmen, whose incomes had for many years been greatly in excess of the value of their services. Scores of conductors have declared since, that in those days they made frequently as much as eight or ten shillings a day beyond their wages, and that, too, after they had paid their coachman his share of the plunder. The companies and proprietors were well aware that the men had been in the habit of keeping back a portion of the daily earnings, but it is doubtful whether they knew the extent to which the practice had grown, for 'busmen, before the strike, were too cautious to talk of what they earned. It was only years after that they began to speak regretfully, and yet with pride, of the prosperous days which preceded the introduction of the ticket system. However, the companies and proprietors promised the men an increase in their wages, to atone for the pilferings which had been winked at. But the additional money promised—two shillings a day—did not make the men's income anything like as large as that to which they were accustomed, and, in their wrath, they vowed to strike. On the night of Saturday, May 6, 1891, after the majority of omnibuses had finished running, large meetings of 'busmen were held in various parts of London, and, amidst intense enthusiasm, the men pledged themselves not to return to work until their grievance had been satisfied. The following morning the strike began all over London, the Road

Car men, who were scarcely interested in the matter, seeing that they had used tickets for years, ceasing work also. Some men remained loyal to their employers, but their efforts to take out their omnibuses were frustrated by the angry mobs of strikers gathered around the stable gates. Day after day the strike dragged on, and for a week the London streets looked quite unfamiliar—devoid of the omnibuses which lend so much life to them. Pirates, of course, did not cease work, but they were comparatively few in number, and were scarcely noticed. Every day the pirates contributed to the strike fund, conscious that the longer the strike lasted, the more profitable it would be for them. It did not, however, last nearly so long as they had hoped, for, on Sunday, May 14, the majority of the men returned to work—and to begin issuing tickets.

But the men who did not go back to work decided to start a Company of their own. It was called the London Co-operative Omnibus Company, and all the conductors, coachmen, and horsekeepers employed by it were to be shareholders in the venture. It started operations with one omnibus, which created a little sensation in the streets by having a broom fixed conspicuously at its fore. This broom was a public intimation of the new Company's intention to sweep the London General, the Road Car and other companies and associations off the roads. But, in spite of its boldness, the London Co-operative Omnibus Company did not prosper. That single omnibus never had a companion, and, after a brief career, it disappeared from the roads, and was bought, it is rumoured, by one of the big companies it was intended to smash.

Shortly after the strike a clergyman, named Jenkins, who had gained considerable notoriety by, among other eccentricities, persistently refusing to show his ticket to tramway inspectors, turned his attention to omnibuses. But as omnibus inspectors have not the power to compel a passenger to show his ticket, Mr. Jenkins was able to enjoy himself with impunity. However, after many quarrels with 'busmen about various trivial matters, he hit, eventually, upon a real grievance. On nearly all omnibuses a long narrow board bearing some advertisement, such as "To Swan and Edgar's," was fixed, outside, across the middle of the side windows. Mr. Jenkins, declared, with truth, that the boards obstructed the view of passengers inside the omnibus, and thereby frequently caused them to be carried beyond the place where they wished to alight. On the same grounds he denounced the transparent advertisements stuck on the side and front windows. His complaint was warmly supported by the public, and the objectionable boards, together with the advertisements on the front windows, were ordered to be removed. The front window advertisements had been abolished but a very short time when the police authorities compelled the proprietors to block up those windows by placing on them the route the omnibus travelled. Consequently the state of affairs, as far as the front windows were concerned, was worse than before. These route-bills have since been reduced in size.

While Mr. Jenkins was denouncing omnibus tickets, inspectors and advertisements, a quarrel occurred between the London General Omnibus Company and the Camden Town Omnibus Association. The London General Omnibus Company had become a member of this old-established association many years previously by purchasing the stock and "times" of retiring members, and worked amicably with its fellow proprietors until about 1896, when a difference of opinion arose concerning an extension of a line of omnibuses. The Company severed its connection with the Association, and at once started working in opposition to it by taking omnibuses from the Finsbury Park and London Bridge route and running them on the Camden Town road. This rivalry was continued for several weeks, but eventually the dispute was settled and the Company rejoined the Association. Had the quarrel been protracted the other associations would, in all probability, have sided with the Camden Town body, and Londoners would have witnessed an exciting, although perhaps not very edifying, struggle.

The Camden Town omnibus fight was followed quickly by a more prolonged one on the Putney road. A new line of omnibuses was started by the Era Association — which was formed by certain proprietors not working in conjunction with any of the companies or associations—from Fulham to Charing Cross, *viâ* West Kensington. Each of these omnibuses carried, at first, a red flag, fixed by the side of the coachman, bearing the inscription "No Monopoly." As their fares were considerably cheaper than those of other omnibuses, the London General Omnibus Company and the Road Car Company's men began to oppose them, and some very amusing scenes were witnessed in the Brompton Road and Piccadilly. The Era Association made a stout fight and started omnibuses from Putney to Charing Cross at the exceedingly low price of twopence for the whole distance. For a time these omnibuses scarcely ever made a journey without being full inside and out, but when the two companies lowered their fares to those of the Era there was a great falling off in the number of the latter's passengers. That was, of course, natural, for when the fares were the same in all omnibuses there was no reason for a thrifty person to wait until an "Era" came along. After a protracted struggle the London General Omnibus Company, the Road Car Company, and the Era raised their fares.

The Era Omnibus Association, which still has some omnibuses on the roads, deserves credit for having placed a list of fares outside their vehicles so that would-be passengers could see, before entering, how much they would have to pay. They did so, of course, to show that their fares were lower than those of the two companies, but, nevertheless, it was an innovation which might well be followed by all omnibus companies and proprietors. If omnibuses were compelled to have a list of fares displayed on the nearside panel it would be a great convenience to the public, and would, moreover, do much towards putting an end to "pirates." At present visitors to London do not know until they have entered an omnibus how much they will be charged. If they sit near the doorway they have to trust to the conductor—for they cannot read the fares—and if it be a pirate omnibus they will assuredly be overcharged.

Early in 1899 the Home Secretary, Sir Matthew White Ridley, brought in a Bill for the better regulation of the street traffic of London, which proposed to confer upon the police the power to relieve the congested thoroughfares by diverting omnibuses from them. The Bill was a very unpopular one, and Metropolitan members of the House of Commons were bombarded with letters from their constituents urging them to vote against it. In June Sir J. Blundell Maple, M.P., presented to the Home Secretary a petition signed by over one hundred thousand regular riders praying that the

Street Traffic Bill, then before Parliament, should be altered to preclude the possibility of omnibuses being diverted from the main thoroughfares. Many thousands of signatures were received too late to be included in the monster petition, which was presented in the form of a huge volume. This unpopular Bill was withdrawn and, on October 14, as a compliment to Sir J. Blundell Maple, who had worked hard to obtain such a result, the 'busmen displayed his racing colours on their whips and bell-cords. These favours they exhibited for three days.

In July of the same year the London County Council issued an order that on and after September 1, every omnibus should carry an outside front lamp on the offside. Red, green, blue, and yellow lamps had for many years been displayed by omnibuses running to the more distant suburbs, but these had to be changed for white ones. When September 1 arrived, very few of the omnibuses were provided with the necessary lamps, the demand for which was greater than the supply. Some days' grace was allowed, and eventually every omnibus carried an outside lamp.

# CHAPTER X

The Motor Traction Company's omnibus—An electric omnibus—The Central London Railway—The London County Council omnibuses—The "corridor 'bus"—The latest omnibus struggle—Present omnibus routes

On October 9, 1899, the Motor Traction Company, Limited, placed an oil-motor omnibus on the roads. No horseless omnibus had been licensed in London for over sixty years, and, naturally, considerable interest was taken in the new venture. A trial run over the course, from Kennington Park to Victoria Station, *viâ* Westminster Bridge, had been made a week earlier. On that occasion the weather was very unpropitious, but the passengers were cheerful and drank success to the trip in a glass of wine. Then, midst cheers and blowing of trumpets, the motor omnibus started on its journey. It was a successful run, and, as already stated, on October 9, the omnibus began to earn money.

In appearance it resembled an ordinary omnibus

robbed of its horses and pole. The driver had a covered seat low down in the front. The body of the vehicle was painted white, and the lower and storage part blue. While the omnibus was travelling no great fault could be found with it, but its warmest admirers could not say truthfully that when it stopped the sensation was pleasant. It vibrated abominably, and when I had my first ride on it, I echoed inwardly the hope expressed by a fellow-passenger that there was no bilious person present.

In the spring of 1900 the motor omnibus was running from Kennington to Oxford Circus, but, towards the end of the year, it disappeared from the London streets.

Some months before the Motor Traction Company's omnibus was placed on the roads an electric 'bus, belonging to a company which was being floated, ran, on many afternoons, from Marble Arch to Notting-hill Gate. It was not licensed, and therefore all rides were free. This omnibus carried no outside passengers, an omission which would have doomed it to failure had it entered into competition with other omnibuses.

The proprietors of horse-drawn omnibuses have

been accused of want of enterprise because they have not yet adopted motor vehicles, against which they are said to have a prejudice. But these accusations are absurd. Omnibus proprietors are convinced that when a really reliable electric 'bus has been invented, it will pay them to adopt it. So far that omnibus has not been discovered, although for two or three years the proprietors have examined carefully every vehicle brought before them.

In the spring of 1900 the Central London Railway was opened, and proved to be the most formidable rival that omnibuses have had since the introduction of tramways. The new electric railway runs from Shepherd's Bush to the Bank, the fare for the whole journey being twopence. The omnibus fare for the same distance was fivepence. The London General Omnibus Company, which has practically a monopoly of the road between Shepherd's Bush and Marble Arch, soon felt the effects of the Central London Railway's cheap fares and quick travelling, and found it necessary to transfer many of their Shepherd's Bush omnibuses to other routes.

With other electric railways projected, it is said,

by some people, that the long-continued prosperity of omnibuses is drawing to a close. There seems, however, to be no real reason for such an assertion. The District and Metropolitan Railways, when first opened, inflicted greater damage to the omnibuses than the Central London has done, and yet to-day their directors complain of omnibus competition. Railway directors bemoaning omnibus competition! Shillibeer was not, after all, wrong in believing that omnibuses could compete successfully with a railway.

The prosperity of electric railways by no means implies ruin to omnibuses. In fact, omnibus proprietors will, no doubt, before long, regard electric railways as their benefactors, for having removed a difficulty which has faced them for many years. The rapid growth of the population of London has made it necessary for the number of omnibuses to be increased every year, but the streets are already uncomfortably crowded with vehicles, and it will be impossible to continue adding to them at the same rate as heretofore. The electric railways, by carrying a portion of the public, will make an increase of omnibuses unnecessary.

The Central London Railway is not, however,

the only formidable rival of omnibus proprietors which has recently sprung into existence. In 1898 the London County Council, authorised by the Tramways Act of 1896, took over the business of the London Tramways Company, Limited. This company, having failed to obtain statutory powers to run their trams over Blackfriars, Waterloo, and Westminster Bridges, started a service of halfpenny omnibuses connecting their termini with, respectively, Farringdon Road, Somerset House, and Trafalgar Square. The London County Council, on taking over the trams, extended the two latter omnibus routes by running their vehicles along the Strand, thus connecting their tram terminus south of Westminster Bridge with the terminus south of Waterloo Bridge. Until then the lowest fare for a ride along the Strand was a penny, but the County Council omnibuses took passengers from Trafalgar Square over Waterloo Bridge for a halfpenny. Naturally they were well patronised, and the old-established omnibus proprietors found an alarming decrease in their profits. The two big omnibus companies were the smallest sufferers by this competition. The London Road Car Company has no omnibuses crossing the bridges referred to, and the London General Omnibus Company is less represented in the south of London than in any other part of the metropolis. The action of the County Council was, therefore, felt chiefly by individual proprietors, who objected strongly to the rates, to which they contributed, being used for the purpose of injuring their business. They contended that the County Council had no more right to become omnibus proprietors than they had to start business as linen drapers or tobacconists, and, after taking counsel's opinion, sought an injunction to put a stop to the competition. Mr. Justice Cozens Hardy decided that the County Council were only authorised to purchase and work tramways, and as they could not confine their omnibuses to tramway passengers—for omnibuses came under the regulation applying to hackney-carriages, and were bound to take any passenger who paid his fare—their service was unlawful. He refused to grant an injunction pending the hearing of an appeal, but ordered the London County Council to pay the costs of the action.

In the Appeal Court, Lords Justices Rigby, Vaughan-Williams and Stirling held that the

Council had no power to run the omnibuses, and dismissed the appeal with costs. An injunction was granted restraining the London County Council from continuing the omnibuses, the operation of the injunction being, however, suspended, provided that notice of an appeal to the House of Lords was given within a month.

After this decision the proprietors offered to take over the London County Council omnibuses and run them at the same fares and times, but the offer was declined and the appeal was carried to the House of Lords. At the time of writing the appeal has not been heard.

To the London County Council belongs the credit of having started all-night omnibuses, which were a great boon to many scores of workers in Fleet Street and Covent Garden. It may, however, be taken for granted that the venture was not a profitable one.

A new omnibus, called "the corridor 'bus,' was placed on the Putney and Liverpool Street road in 1900, by Mr. William Berg. From the outside the vehicle appears to be similar to the ordinary omnibus, but the inside seats are arranged crossways and some of the passengers sit back to back. The windows are fitted with blinds—a much-needed innovation. I have heard that one of the smaller omnibus companies intends to adopt "the corridor 'bus."

One of the keenest struggles between rival omnibus companies that has been witnessed for some years began in May last. It originated in the following way:—some twelve years ago the London General Omnibus Company opened a line of omnibuses from Kilburn to the Redcliffe Arms, Fulham Road. These omnibuses, which were painted blue, tapped Harrow Road, Westbourne Grove, Notting Hill Gate, Kensington High Street, and Earl's Court, and, before long, the line became one of the best patronised in London. But about a week before Whit Monday the London Road Car Company started a service of twenty-five orange-coloured omnibuses from Putney to Brondesbury, which traversed the entire route of the blue 'buses. The London General Omnibus Company immediately extended the journey of some of its "blues," making them run from Brondesbury to Putney, and its drivers at once began to oppose their "orange" rivals. The London Road Car Company then displayed in its omnibuses a "No Monopoly" protest, stating that a determined attempt was being made to run its cars off the road, and appealing to the public to "rally round the flag." A few weeks later a leaflet, headed "No Surrender!" was distributed in the districts through which the "oranges" and "blues" passed. It bore an illustration of a smart, well-patronised Putney and Brondesbury Road Car being followed by an almost empty knife-board omnibus. Beneath this amusing, but somewhat misleading, illustration were the following lines:—

"Welcome, welcome London Road-Car, beard the mammoth God of
Shares,
Pioneers of all improvements, handsome cars and cheaper fares;
No more 'tubs' and foreign gee-gees, onward, Road-Car, spread the
light,
No more sixpence any distance after eight on Sunday night.

"'No more turning back,' said Buller, to the gallant rank and file;
No white flag was ever hoisted by the 'Dubs' from Erin's isle;
Strike no flag, and give no quarter, for with them it's 'outing-dues,'
Good luck to the 'orange blossoms,' for we've long since had the 'blues.'

"Stand no nursing, Road-Car drivers, you've a right as well as they,
Forward, valiant standard-bearers, bravo "D" and "B" and "J."
Come to stay's the public verdict, bull-dog pluck cannot be beat,
Men and masters, pull together, no surrender! no retreat!

"To the public I'm appealing; forward help this gallant band,
'Neath the grand old flag of England in your thousands take your stand;
Trace to them all known improvements, now, as in the days of yore,
When a change is really needed, they'll send five-and-twenty more."

"Cead a Mille Failthe."

"D" and "B" and "J" are Mr. Duff, the manager of the Road Car Company, and Messrs. Bristow and Jones, two other officials.

The London Road Car Company has certainly, during its comparatively short career, been more enterprising than its rivals in providing for the comfort of the omnibus-travelling public; but it is scarcely entitled to much sympathy in connection with the Putney and Brondesbury struggle, considering that, not many years ago, it meted out to a small company treatment similar to that of which it now complains. It compelled that company—which also issued an appeal to the public—to submit to its terms, in spite of the fact that, unlike the London General Omnibus Company and other companies who are members of the various associations, it does not pay compensation for placing its omnibuses on a route which another company has planned and worked into success.

It is somewhat surprising that the London General Omnibus Company and the proprietors associated with it have not thought it advisable to publish periodically, for the convenience of the public, a list of their routes. Visitors to London are frequently in need of such a guide. The following is a list of omnibus lines which run through or into London.

Acton and Charing Cross (*viâ* Shepherd's Bush, Bayswater Road, Oxford Street, and Regent Street).

Baker-street Station and Victoria (*viâ* Baker Street, Grosvenor Square, and Hyde Park Corner).

Baker-street Station and Waterloo (*viâ* Baker Street, Bond Street, and Westminster Bridge).

Barnes and Uxbridge Road (*viâ* Hammersmith Broadway).

Barnes Common and Liverpool Street (*viâ* Putney Bridge, Walham Green, Brompton Road, Piccadilly, and Strand).

Barnsbury and Brixton (*viâ* Liverpool Road, General Post Office, and Blackfriars Bridge).

Battersea and South Hackney (*viâ* King's Road, Chelsea, Sloane Street, Piccadilly, Strand, Bank, and Bethnal-green Road).

Blackwall and Piccadilly Circus (*viâ* Commercial Road, Shoreditch, Bank, and Strand).

Bow and Oxford Circus (*viâ* Mile End Road, Bank, and Strand).

Brixton and Gracechurch Street (*viâ* Kennington and London Bridge).

Brixton and Oxford Circus (*viâ* Kennington, Westminster Bridge, and Piccadilly Circus).

Brixton and Paddington Station (*viâ* Kennington, Elephant and Castle, Blackfriars Bridge, Gray's-inn Road, Euston Road, and Marylebone Road).

Camberwell and Camden Town (*viâ* Elephant and Castle, Waterloo Bridge, Strand, Oxford Circus, and Portland Road.

Camberwell and Clapham Common (*viâ* Loughboro' Junction and Brixton).

Camberwell and King's Cross (*viâ* Elephant and Castle, Waterloo Bridge, and Gray's-inn Road).

Camberwell and Shoreditch Church (*viâ* Elephant and Castle, London Bridge, and Liverpool-street Station).

Camden Town and Kent Road (*viâ* Elephant and Castle, Waterloo Bridge, Strand, Oxford Circus, and Portland Road).

Chalk Farm and Victoria (*viâ* Hampstead Road, Tottenham-court Road, Charing Cross, and Victoria Street).

Child's Hill and Charing Cross (*viâ* Finchley Road, Baker Street, Wigmore Street, Oxford Circus, and Piccadilly Circus).

Clapham Common and Victoria (*viâ* Battersea Bridge and Buckingham-palace Road).

Clapham Junction and Hyde Park (*viâ* Albert Bridge, King's Road, Chelsea, and Sloane Street).

Clapham Junction and Shepherd's Bush (*viâ* Albert Bridge, King's Road, Sloane Street, Kensington Church, and Notting-hill Gate).

Clapton and Elephant and Castle (*viâ* Dalston Junction, Kingsland Road, Shoreditch, and London Bridge).

Clapton and Finsbury-park Station (*viâ* Stoke Newington, Green Lanes, and Brownswood Park).

Cricklewood and Charing Cross (*viâ* Kilburn, Oxford Circus, and Piccadilly Circus).

Ealing and Tottenham-court Road (*viâ* Acton, Shepherd's Bush, Bayswater Road, and Oxford Street).

Earl's Court and Elephant and Castle (*viâ* Cromwell Road, Sloane Street, Victoria Station, Vauxhall Bridge, and Kennington).

Elephant and Castle and Islington (*viâ* London Bridge, Bank, General Post Office, and Goswell Road).

Farringdon Road and Blackfriars Bridge (*viâ* Ludgate Circus).

Finchley and Charing Cross (*viâ* East Finchley, Highgate Archway, Junction Road, Camden Town, Hampstead Road, and Tottenham-court Road).

Finchley and Oxford Circus (*viâ* Church End, Child's Hill, Swiss Cottage, Baker Street, and Wigmore Street).

Finchley Road (North Star) and Fulham Road (*viâ* Kilburn, Harrow Road, Westbourne Grove, Notting-hill Gate, Kensington, and Earl's-court Road).

Finsbury Park and Kent Road (*viâ* Highbury Barn, Upper Street, New North Road, Bank, and Elephant and Castle).

Finsbury Park and Victoria (*viâ* Seven Sisters' Road, Camden Road, Hampstead Road, Tottenham-court Road, Charing Cross, and Victoria Street).

Fulham and Bethnal Green (*viâ* Walham Green, King's Road, Chelsea, Sloane Square, Victoria Station, Whitehall, Strand, and Bank).

Fulham and Liverpool Street (as above).

Fulham and Oxford Circus (*viâ* King's Road, Chelsea, Sloane Street, and Piccadilly).

Gospel Oak and Victoria (*viâ* Ferdinand Road, Hampstead Road, Charing Cross, and Victoria Street).

Gower-street Station and Edgware-road Station (*viâ* Tottenham-court Road, Oxford Street, and Edgware Road).

Hammersmith and Caledonian Road (*viâ* Kensington, Piccadilly, Tottenham Court Road, and Euston Road).

Hammersmith and Liverpool Street (*viâ* Kensington, Piccadilly, Strand, and Bank).

Hammersmith and Walham Green (*viâ* Fulham).

Hammersmith and Wandsworth (*viâ* Fulham, Walham Green, and Wandsworth Bridge).

Hampstead and Oxford Street (*viâ* Haverstock Hill, Hampstead Road, and Tottenham-court Road).

Hanwell and Oxford Circus (*viâ* Ealing, Acton, Shepherd's Bush, Bayswater Road, and Oxford Street).

Harlesden and Charing Cross (*viâ* Kensal Green, Harrow Road, Paddington Station, Edgware Road, and Oxford Circus).

Hendon and Oxford Circus (*viâ* Golder's Hill, Child's Hill, St. John's Wood, Baker-street Station, and Wigmore Street).

Highbury Barn and Putney Bridge (*viâ* Upper Street, Rosebery Avenue, Shaftesbury Avenue, Piccadilly, Sloane Street, King's Road, and Parsons Green).

Highgate and London Bridge (*viâ* Holloway Road, Upper Street, and City Road).

Highgate and Victoria (*viâ* Junction Road, Camden Town, Tottenham-court Road, Charing Cross, and Victoria Street).

Holloway and Bayswater (*viâ* Camden Road, St. John's-wood Road, Maida Vale, Westbourne Grove, and Queen's Road).

Holloway and Fulham (*viâ* Caledonian Road, Euston Road, Portland Road Station, Oxford Circus, Piccadilly, South Kensington and West Kensington).

Hornsey Rise and Sloane Square (*viâ* Islington, Euston Road, Baker Street, Park Lane and Sloane Street).

Hornsey Rise and Victoria (*viâ* Seven Sisters' Road, Upper Street, Gray's-inn Road, Chancery Lane, Strand, and Victoria Street).

Islington and Kensington (*viâ* Pentonville Road, Euston Road, Marylebone Road, Westbourne Grove, and Notting-hill Gate).

Kensal Green and London Bridge (*viâ* Harrow Road, Paddington Station, Edgware Road, Oxford Street, Holborn, and Bank).

Kentish Town and Elephant and Castle (*viâ* College Road, Gray's-inn Road, Holborn, and Blackfriars Bridge).

Kentish Town and London Bridge (*viâ* College Road, Gray's-inn Road, and Holborn).

Kilburn and Charing Cross (*viâ* Maida Vale, Oxford Street, and Regent Street).

Kilburn and Liverpool Street (*viâ* Maida Vale, Oxford Street, Holborn, and Bank).

Kilburn and London Bridge (*viâ* Maida Vale, Oxford Street, Holborn, and Bank).

Kilburn and Victoria (*viâ* Maida Vale, Edgware Road, and Park Lane).

Kilburn and Willesden Junction (*viâ* Willesden Lane and Harlesden).

Knightsbridge and Battersea Bridge (*viâ* Sloane Street).

Mile End and West Brompton (*viâ* Bank, Holborn, Shaftesbury Avenue, Piccadilly, and Brompton Road).

Moorgate-street Station and London-bridge Station (*viâ* Bank).

Muswell Hill and Charing Cross (*viâ* Highgate Archway, Camden Town, and Tottenham-court Road).

Notting Hill and Liverpool Street (*viâ* Westbourne Grove, Paddington Station, Oxford Street, Holborn, and Bank).

Notting Hill and London Bridge (*viâ* Portobello Road, Westbourne Grove, Paddington Station, Oxford Street, Regent Street, Strand, and Cannon Street).

Old Ford and Bank (*viâ* Bethnal-green Road, and Shoreditch).

Old Ford and Oxford Circus (*viâ* Bethnal-green Road, Bank, and Holborn).

Paddington Station and London Bridge (*viâ* Praed Street, Edgware Road, Oxford Street, Regent Street, and Strand).

Peckham and Oxford Circus (*viâ* Camberwell, Westminster Bridge, and Regent Street).

Peckham and Victoria (*viâ* Camberwell, Kennington, and Vauxhall Bridge).

Putney and Brondesbury (*viâ* Fulham Road, Earl's Court Road, Kensington, Notting-hill Gate, Westbourne Grove, Harrow Road, and Kilburn).

Putney and Liverpool Street (*viâ* Walham Green, Brompton Road, Piccadilly, Strand, and Bank).

St. John's Wood and Camberwell (*viâ* Baker Street, Oxford Street, Regent Street, Westminster Bridge, and Elephant and Castle).

St. John's Wood and Kent Road (as above).

St. John's Wood and London Bridge (*viâ* Baker Street, Oxford Street, Holborn, and Bank).

Shepherd's Bush, and Burdett Road, Mile End (*viâ* Bayswater Road, Oxford Street, Holborn, Bank, and Mile-end Road).

Shepherd's Bush and Liverpool Street (*viâ* Bayswater Road, Oxford Street, Holborn, and Bank).

Shepherd's Bush and Walham Green (*viâ* Olympia and West Kensington).

South Hackney and Bank (*viâ* Hackney Road).

Stamford Hill and Elephant and Castle (*viâ* Kingsland Road, Shoreditch, Bank, and London Bridge).

Starch Green and Liverpool Street (*viâ* Shepherd's Bush, Bayswater Road, Oxford Street, Holborn, and Bank).

Stoke Newington and Victoria (*viâ* Newington Green, Essex Road, Angel, Gray's-inn Road, Chancery Lane, Strand, and Victoria Street).

Summer's Town and Hammersmith (*viâ* Earlsfield, Wandsworth Bridge, and Walham Green).

Tollington Park and London Bridge (*viâ* Seven Sisters' Road, Upper Street, City Road, and Bank).

Tollington Park and Victoria (*viâ* Seven Sisters' Road, Upper Street, Gray's-inn Road, Chancery Lane, Strand, and Victoria Street). Another route (*viâ* King's Cross, Bond Street, and Piccadilly).

Tulse Hill and King's Cross (*viâ* Herne Hill, Loughboro' Junction, Camberwell Green, Elephant and Castle, Waterloo Bridge, Chancery Lane, and Gray's Inn Road).

Turnham Green and Clapham Junction (*viâ* Goldhawk Road, Bayswater Road, Notting-hill Gate, Kensington Church, and Sloane Street).

Turnham Green and Liverpool Street (*viâ* Hammersmith Broadway, Kensington, Piccadilly, Strand, and Bank).

Victoria and King's Cross (*viâ* Hyde Park Corner, Piccadilly, Long Acre, Southampton Row, and Russell Square). Another route (*viâ* Hyde Park Corner, Piccadilly, Bond Street, Oxford Street, Tottenham-court Road, and Euston Road).

Victoria and Liverpool Street (*viâ* Victoria Street, Strand, Fleet Street, and Bank).

Walham Green and Islington (*viâ* Brompton Road, Piccadilly, Regent Street, Portland-road Station, Euston Road, and Pentonville Road).

Walham Green and Highbury (*viâ* Piccadilly, Euston Road, Pentonville Road, and Upper Street).

Wandsworth and Liverpool Street (*viâ* King's Road, Chelsea, Victoria, Strand, and Bank).

Waterloo Station and Liverpool Street (*viâ* Blackfriars Bridge and Bank).

Waterloo Station and Westminster Bridge (*viâ* Strand).

Westbourne Grove and Victoria (*viâ* Praed Street, Edgware Road, and Park Lane).

West Hampstead and Elephant and Castle (*viâ* Abbey Road, Eyre Arms, Baker Street, Oxford Street, Regent Street, and Westminster Bridge).

West Hampstead and Fulham Road (*viâ* Kilburn, Westbourne Grove, Notting-hill Gate, Kensington, and Earl's-court Road).

West Kensington and London Bridge (*viâ* South Kensington, Brompton Road, Piccadilly, Holborn, and Bank).

West Kensington and Shoreditch (*viâ* South Kensington, Strand, Bank, and Liverpool Street).

West Kilburn and Charing Cross (*viâ* Shirland Road, Edgware Road, Oxford Street, and Regent Street).

West Kilburn and London Bridge (*viâ* Shirland Road, Edgware Road, Oxford Street, Holborn, and Bank).

West Kilburn and Victoria (*viâ* Shirland Road, Edgware Road, and Park Lane).

West Norwood and Oxford Circus (*viâ* Kennington, Westminster Bridge, and Piccadilly Circus).

Westminster and Liverpool Street (*viâ* Moreton Street, Great Smith Street, Whitehall, Strand, and Bank).

Willesden and Charing Cross (*viâ* Willesden Lane, Salusbury Road, Shirland Road, Edgware Road, and Oxford Street).

Willesden and Victoria (*viâ* Willesden Lane, Salusbury Road, Shirland Road, Edgware Road, and Park Lane).

Wormwood Scrubbs and Liverpool Street (*viâ* Notting Hill, Westbourne Grove, Praed Street, Oxford Street, Holborn, and Bank).

Wormwood Scrubbs and London Bridge (*viâ* Notting Hill, Westbourne Grove, Praed Street, Oxford Street, Holborn, and Bank).

During the summer months many omnibuses are taken off the City Roads on Sundays, and run into the suburbs. The chief of these Sunday routes are :—

Bank and Romford Road (*viâ* Bow and Stratford).

Charing Cross and Richmond (*viâ* Kensington, Hammersmith, Chiswick, and Kew Bridge).

Kensal Green and Richmond (*viâ* Shepherd's Bush, Barnes, Mortlake).

Oxford Circus and Hayes Common (*viâ* Shepherd's Bush, Acton, Ealing, and Hanwell).

Oxford Circus and Welsh Harp (*viâ* Kilburn and Cricklewood).

Stoke Newington and Hadley Woods (*viâ* Wood Green and Southgate).

Tottenham-court Road and Stonebridge Park (*viâ* Kensal Green and Harlesden).

# CHAPTER XI

"Jumpers"—"Spots"—Some curious passengers—Conductors and coachmen—The Rothschild Christmas-boxes—Mr. Morris Abrahams and Omnibus Men's Superannuation Fund—Horses—Cost of omnibuses—Night in an omnibus yard

It is said, frequently, that omnibus companies and proprietors have received little or no benefit from the introduction of the ticket system because of the expense connected with the working of it, but that is a very great mistake. The London General Omnibus Company saves £100,000 a year by it, and the other companies and associations have just as much cause for satisfaction. But it must be confessed that at the outset the ticket system was more or less a farce, the conductors omitting openly to give tickets and being encouraged in their breach of duty by the lower class of riders. Some conductors flung away their rolls of tickets and declared that they had been stolen. Others placed them under the omnibus wheels to be crushed, and then pretended that the damage done was the result of an accident. Some of the more reckless spirits bragged that they had given the tickets to their children to play with.

The polite inspectors—called by the men "jumpers"—came into existence with the introduction of tickets, and for some time there was a considerable amount of excitement about their work, for, while conductors did not trouble to conceal from passengers the fact that they were not doing their duty, they seemed to consider it a personal insult that an inspector should board their omnibuses to see if passengers had been given tickets. Some conductors assaulted the unwelcome inspectors, but the police-court magistrates soon proved to them that it was a very unprofitable step to take, and, in course of time, the men who wished to retain their posts settled down to issuing tickets in a proper fashion, and to regarding with comparative calmness the sudden appearance of an inspector on their step.

"We have to punch tickets in the dark," one conductor declared indignantly to a passenger, "and then a 'jumper' comes up with an electric light to see that we've punched them in the right section."

"Perhaps they'll fix electric lights on top of the 'buses before long," the passenger said, consolingly.

"Hope they won't, guv'nor," the conductor answered hurriedly. "Shouldn't get any more two-shilling pieces for pennies if they did."

Ticket-inspectors are known to all Londoners, but few people are aware that the omnibus companies have also private inspectors, whose duty it is to ride about in their omnibuses, as ordinary passengers, for the purpose of noting and reporting anything that affects their interests adversely. These people, who are called "spots" and "wrong 'uns" by the 'busmen, are not beloved by conductors and coachmen, for the simple reason that they never know when they have one on their omnibus. The man in evening dress who enters the omnibus in the Strand after the theatres have closed may be one; so, too, may be the man with a bag of workman's tools who rides up to town by the first omnibus. The daintily dressed young lady who enters at Peter Robinson's or William Whiteley's may, from her seat in the corner, be regarding the conductor with an interest which is not born of admiration, and the palpably retired officer who gets in at Piccadilly may be earning a welcome addition to his income by watching 'busmen's manœuvres. But it must be very embarrassing to these "spots" as they sit, unobtrusively, in the omnibus to see facing them, as an advertisement of Sapolio, Lady Macbeth's exhortation, "Out, out, damned spot!"

Private inspectors are by no means a modern addition to the staff of an omnibus company. Shillibeer, as stated in Chapter II., employed them a few weeks after he placed the first English omnibuses on the road, and succeeding omnibus proprietors followed his example. The duties of these early inspectors were not very arduous, for, as there were only shilling and sixpenny fares, known as "longs" and "shorts," and but two outside seats, it was a simple matter to check the amount received by a conductor during a journey. The defalcations of conductors were, by the means of these inspectors, kept from being extensive, but when omnibuses had been in existence about fifteen years one of the largest proprietors received reports from his "spot" which he could not understand. The "spot" would state that a certain omnibus, on a certain journey, had carried, say, twelve "longs" and sixteen "shorts," but the conductor would pay in the fares of fourteen "longs" and seventeen or eighteen "shorts." To unravel this mystery the proprietor persuaded a relation, who was unknown to the 'busmen, to ride in a certain omnibus on the same journey as his "spot," and check who was really right. This man's reports agreed with the "spot's." Both declared that the conductor had collected less money than he paid in. The amateur "spot" then rode two journeys in that omnibus when the professional man was not there, and on those occasions it was found that the conductor paid in only about three-quarters of the money he received. Eventually the conductor was arrested for fraud, and confessed how he had been working his omnibus. He had bribed the proprietor's clerk to tell him who the "spot" was, and where he could be seen. As soon as he had received that information, and taken a good look at the man, he felt that he was safe from being detected in his fraud. Whenever the "spot" rode in his omnibus, he paid in more than he received, relying upon getting back the extra money, and a good bit more, on the journeys when the "spot" was not present. Why he did not remain satisfied with simply paying in the exact amount he took on every occasion that the "spot" rode in his omnibus is a question that occurs to every one who hears the story. In all probability he considered himself a very smart fellow, and it is the fate of people possessed of an exaggerated idea of their own cleverness to make some silly blunder which proves that, after all, they are but fools.

In the forties and fifties several well-dressed women "spots" were employed by the omnibus proprietors, and when a conductor suspected any lady passenger of being one, he generally communicated his suspicion to the coachman, with the result that when she wished to alight, the coachman would pull up in the muddiest part of the road, so that she would be compelled to get her boots and skirt dirty. More often than not it was a perfectly innocent lady whom the conductor left stranded in the centre of a crowded, muddy street. These mistakes are still very common. Conductors are always on the look out for "spots," and every day hundreds of innocent passengers are suspected of being private inspectors because they happen, perhaps unconsciously, to watch the conductor punching tickets or to glance at his badge number.

Although private inspectors are, naturally enough, very strongly disliked by 'busmen, they are a great protection to them. There are always a few cantankerous, cross-grained people riding in omnibuses somewhere in London who abuse conductors with scarcely any reason, and threaten, when they have aggravated them into retort, to report them for impertinence. And sometimes they do report the man, but if a "spot" happens to be in the omnibus he sends to his employers a full account of all that occurred. He does not forget to mention the provocation the conductor received, a point which people who write letters of complaint have a curious knack of overlooking.

Sometimes conductors get very strange people in their omnibuses. One night, a year or two ago, a "Favorite" started from Victoria Station with three inside passengers, two of whom were women. Suddenly the woman sitting by the door pointed at the one at the other end of the omnibus and exclaimed dramatically :—

"That woman has stolen my purse."

"She hasn't been near you," the conductor declared ; but the woman repeated the accusation in a louder tone.

The accused woman remained very calm, and it was not until the charge against her began to get monotonous through repetition that she told the conductor to stop the omnibus and call a policeman. The conductor did so.

"That woman has stolen my purse," the passenger at the door shouted when the policeman arrived.

The policeman looked from one to the other, and then said:—

"Why, there's your purse in your lap."

"Yes, I know," the accuser admitted.

"Then, what do you mean by sayin' that lady stole it?"

"I did it out of kindness, constable. The lady has got the hiccoughs, and I wanted to give her a start."

To be accused of having the hiccoughs seemed to annoy the woman in the corner far more than the charge of theft did, and she appealed, excitedly, to the male passenger to say whether or not she had the hiccoughs. He answered boldly that there was not the slightest ground for such an accusation.

"But she was going to have them," the woman by the door declared, an assertion which so astonished the policeman that he felt prompt action was imperative.

"Out you come," he said sharply, and assisted her to make her exit with alacrity.

At times the eccentricity of some passengers takes very objectionable forms. Quite recently a well-dressed little woman jumped into an omnibus in Fleet Street, pulled a man out of his seat and sat in it herself, poked her umbrella into another man's eye, swore horribly at everybody present for about half a minute, then suddenly got up, jumped out without paying, and disappeared down a side street. The man whose eye was injured had to hurry to Charing Cross Hospital.

On another occasion a sane-looking man, sitting on top of an omnibus, suddenly started throwing pennies at the silk hats of passers-by and spitting contemptuously at female pedestrians. Before his fellow-passengers had made up their minds whether to pitch him off the omnibus or give him into custody, he walked quietly down the steps and alighted.

Many passengers leave strange things in omnibuses, but I have heard of only one man who went away without his clothes. A conductor looking round his omnibus at the end of his day's work, kicked against a heap of clothes lying on the roof. While examining the articles by the light of his lamp he heard a noise above him, and, looking up, beheld a man, stark naked, climbing into the loft. The poor fellow had gone mad.

But of all the eccentric characters known to 'busmen, the most harmless and the most amusing is the respectable-looking little man with a black beard who runs in front of omnibuses, excitedly waving a long stick above his head. He is about forty years of age, dressed generally in black clothes, and sometimes carries a pair of gloves in his hand. He singles out an omnibus, gives a friendly shout to the coachman, darts in front of the horses, and leads the way through the streets, coming occasionally to the side of the omnibus to give passengers an opportunity to throw money to him. He delights in long runs and usually sticks to the omnibus he takes up with until it reaches the end of its journey. He has been known to run with an omnibus from Queen's Road, Bayswater, through the city, to Burdett Road, E., and then to run back with another.

An eccentric person, well known to 'busmen in one part of London, is a gentleman who stands, almost every night, at certain corners where omnibuses stop and gives a searching look at each one as it comes up. When he started that practice, ten or fifteen years ago, the 'busmen thought that he was some omnibus official, but they soon discovered that he was not. Who or what he has been looking for all these years neither 'busmen, policemen, nor any one else, know. Sometimes conductors say to him, "Coming our way, sir?" Whereupon he answers sharply, "Take your departure." Usually he allows about a hundred omnibuses to pass before he enters one, but sometimes he lets the last go by and then walks home.

Omnibus conductors are, on the whole, a very respectable and intelligent class of men, and this is scarcely to be wondered at, for their pay, after one year's service, is six shillings a day. These wages cause hundreds of clerks and shopmen to resign their positions and become conductors. Many men who have been in business for themselves, but failed to earn a good living, are to be seen wearing the conductor's badge and punch.

The army, it is pleasing to be able to say, is very well represented—largely by ex-noncommissioned officers. They do not wear their medals on their waistcoats, because they know that to be the practice of old soldiers in straitened circumstances, and also, alas! of rascally impostors who have never worn the Queen's uniform. If the conductors had uniforms, as the tram-men have, they would wear their medals.

The dissipated down-at-heel gentleman, of the type which sometimes drives a cab, never becomes an omnibus conductor, for the very good reason that no company or proprietor would employ him. But the unfortunate gentleman often does. An Oxford graduate was the conductor of a West-End omnibus for some considerable time, and a man who was once the secretary of a flourishing literary society, and a church organist, is and has been one for some years. And a City man, ruined in business, became, by the irony of fate, the conductor of the very omnibus on which he, formerly, rode up to town every morning.

A small proportion of conductors do possibly make occasional mistakes in their grammar, but that is no reason why a certain writer should have attributed to them, week after week for some years, a dialect which they do not speak. Evidently the writer has not troubled to study conductors, and imagines that they are drawn from the costermonger class. Conductors, it may be added, do not even say "lidy," or "lydy," although it has become the fashion in novels and articles to make out that they do. They say "lady" as distinctly as ever the word was uttered.

Omnibus drivers are, as a body, intellectually inferior to conductors. They are usually brought up among horses, and, unlike the conductors, are totally unfitted for any other calling than the one by which they earn their living. Their wages, which are eight shillings a day, after one year's service, enable them to live in comfort and to put a shilling on a horse in every race of any importance. They have no ambition but to "back a winner," and many men who started driving at the age of twenty-one are not a penny richer after forty years' regular work. They continue driving until they become too old, and then they realise that they have been exceedingly foolish. One driver, who for more than forty years earned over two guineas a week, now sweeps a crossing for a living. Many others have died in the workhouse.

As a wit the omnibus driver is greatly overrated. There is nothing spontaneous about his witticisms, and all drivers let off exactly the same jokes. These are three from their stock :—

When a coal cart is in front of them : "Now then, short weight, hurry up!"

When another omnibus remains at a point longer than usual : "Got a bit of freeehold there?"

When they are driving home to the stables about midnight, and some would-be passenger hails them : "Not to-night, sir. We have the rest of the evening to ourselves."

But it must be admitted that omnibus drivers have the knack of delivering their remarks in a way that makes a stranger imagine that they are uttering them for the first time. And that is an art.

At Christmas time there is a great demand among 'busmen for Rothschild's racing colours. The drivers attach them to their whips and the conductors adorn their bell-pulls with them, as a slight acknowledgment of the welcome Christmas-box—a brace of pheasants—which they have received for many years from the firm of Rothschild. Originally these presents were given only to the coachmen and conductors of omnibuses which passed the Rothschilds' houses, but now others receive them as well, and there must be about three thousand brace distributed every Christmas.

The late Lord Rothschild, who, years ago, gave an annual dinner to the Hammersmith 'busmen—half the men being entertained on one night and half on another—was the first of the family to present Christmas-boxes to them. His gift to every Hammersmith coachman and conductor was a brace of pheasants, a bottle of wine and six cigars. After a time he stopped the bottle of wine and cigars and gave five shillings instead. The Victoria Station Omnibus Association coachmen and conductors also receive five shillings each as well as the brace of pheasants, and the reason why they are favoured is, the old 'busmen say, as follows:—One day, many years ago, in the height of the season, there was a big crowd gathered in Park Lane, and the traffic was stopped for some time to keep the road clear for a member of the Royal Family to drive along.

By the fountain the block was so great that pedestrians who desired to cross the road experienced the greatest difficulty in doing so. A lady of the Rothschild family came up Hertford Street and wished to cross over into Hamilton Place, but, naturally, did not venture to pick her way through the wide stretch of omnibuses, cabs and carriages. Benjamin West, a conductor of one of the Victoria Station Association's omnibuses, saw her, and, recognising her, got off his step and, with a polite apology for addressing her, asked to be allowed to escort her across the road. His services were accepted, and he led the way safely through the maze of horses and vehicles. West then returned to his omnibus, well satisfied at having been useful to a member of the family which contains the best friends that 'busmen ever had. But, to his surprise, he saw the lady turn and speak to the page following her, in charge of a pug dog, who came running back to West's omnibus to see to whom it belonged. He read the inscription on the panel, "Victoria Station Association," and then hurried back and reported to his mistress. The following Christmas every conductor and coachman in the employ of the Victoria Station

Association received from Mr. Leopold Rothschild five shillings, and the present has been given every year since.

Many instances of the Rothschilds' generosity to individual 'busmen could be given, but it would be indiscreet to mention actions which were performed privately.

The Rothschilds are not, however, the only Jews from whom London 'busmen have received substantial benefits. The late Messrs. Barney Barnato and Woolf Joel were very generous to them, and Mr. Morris Abrahams has placed them under a debt of gratitude by starting, on October 26, 1897, the Omnibus Men's Superannuation Fund. Mr. Abrahams, who is a cousin of the late Mr. Barnato, had for some years taken a kindly interest in the 'busmen of the neighbourhood in which he resides, when he was asked to contribute to a fund being raised for the benefit of an old driver, who was incapacitated from further work. He did as desired, and was present at the meeting at which the money was presented to the 'busman. It struck him, however, that this gift was only postponing the old man's days of poverty. The money would keep him for about eighteen months; at the end of that time the man would be still less able to earn even a few pence. The need of a superannuation fund was so obvious that Mr. Abrahams rose and suggested to the men that they should start one, adding that if they would support the movement he would provide all the money necessary for founding it. The men received the suggestion with cheers, and raising Mr. Abrahams aloft, carried him round the room. Finding that the 'busmen would appreciate a fund of the nature he had suggested, he set to work to start one. His first step was to instruct two men in the employ of the London General Omnibus Company to apply for a week's leave, so that they might go all over London to ask the 'busmen to appoint a man from each district to represent them on the committee. The two men obtained the necessary leave, Mr. Abrahams paying them their usual wages, and expenses, while away from work. The first general meeting was held at the Horse Shoe. Six hundred and thirty 'busmen were present, and £40 was collected from them in subscriptions. Mr. Abrahams, who was in the chair, presented the fund, on behalf of Messrs. Barnato, with £250. From that day the Omnibus

Men's Superannuation Fund has made rapid progress, and has now 1300 members and a reserve of £3200. Mr. Abrahams is the president, Mr. Alfred Rothschild the vice-president, and among the other supporters of the Fund are the Duke of Cambridge, the Duke of Westminster, the Earl of Crewe, Lord Rosebery, and many members of both Houses of Parliament. Mrs. Aubert made a donation of four hundred guineas, and Mr. Woolf Joel left the Fund £250. The trustees are Mr. E. R. P. Moon, M.P., and Mr. Lister Drummond, and the committee is composed of twenty-eight 'busmen; the chairman and vice-chairman are both 'bus drivers. The Fund gives fifteen shillings a week for life to any member incapacitated from following his customary employment. The first recipient was "Fat" Smith, a well-known driver of a Kilburn and Victoria omnibus. In his young days Smith drove a stage-coach in Wales, but coming to London in the sixties he obtained a job as an omnibus driver, and retained it until about three years ago, when old age compelled him to resign. The Fund has twenty-three pensioners in all, and the number will soon be increased.

The theatrical profession has given the Fund valuable aid. Mr. George Alexander lent his theatre for a *matinée*, at which a large number of the best actors and actresses gave their services. The performance lasted from half-past two until six, and hundreds of people were unable to gain admittance. At the conclusion of the performance the old 'busmen went on the stage and bowed their thanks. Mr. Abrahams has received promises of further help from theatrical managers, actors and actresses.

When the Fund had been started a few months the 'busmen decided to present Mr. Abrahams with a testimonial, and had collected £60 with which to purchase it when he heard of their action and communicated to them his intention not to accept the gift. He requested that the money collected should be returned to the subscribers. But four years later the men were determined that he should have a testimonial, and on June 27, 1901, they presented him, at a meeting at the Holborn Restaurant, with an exquisite silver model of an omnibus. Jim Perry, who is eighty-one years of age, and has driven a London omnibus since 1844, is faithfully reproduced as the driver of the presentation omnibus. Perry may be seen any day driving a London General Omnibus Company omnibus between Baker Street and Victoria Stations. The conductor of the silver 'bus represents J. Baker, a Fulham conductor, known as "Sailor Jack," who acts as collector to the Superannuation Fund.

Mr. Abrahams has, without ostentation, given both time and money to the Fund, and it is to be hoped that London 'busmen will never forget their indebtedness to him.

At the present day there are about 3700 omnibuses on the London streets. For each omnibus there is a stud of ten horses, except when the road on which it works is hilly, and then twelve are required. The majority of omnibus horses are Canadians, and are purchased at the London repositories when between five and eight years of age, the average price paid being £30 per horse. They are then graduated to the work, and become seasoned in two or three months. When seasoned they work from four to five hours out of every twenty-four. After working for about five years they are, generally, unfit for further omnibus use, and are sold by auction, the purchasers being, in most cases, farmers. Many horses recover their "straight legs" after a spell of farm life, and farmers have been known to send up to London as English bred horses Canadians which they purchased, some months before, as "fresh from omnibus work." On several occasions omnibus proprietors have discovered that their new "English bred horse" is a Canadian which they had sold, deeming it unfit for further use. It may be asked how it was that the purchaser did not recognise his old horse before buying it. But omnibus proprietors in a large way of business are continually buying horses, and cannot possibly recognise every animal they have possessed; but their horse-foremen, however, discover the British farmer's smartness. In all large studs a number is allotted to every horse as soon as it is purchased. That number is burnt on the near fore hoof, and entered, together with the colour and sex of the animal, in the horse-register book. It is also painted on a slip of zinc and placed over the stall the horse is to occupy. When the animal dies or is sold his number plate is destroyed and a fresh one allotted to his successor.

Each omnibus costs from £150 to £160, and lasts for about twelve years. It is renovated every year previous to being inspected by the police, who, on passing it, affix a number plate to the back of the step. The police have two plates, which they issue on alternate years, so that a constable can see at a glance whether an omnibus is licensed. For each plate licence an omnibus proprietor has to pay £2 a year, and also an annual tax of 15*s*. to the Inland Revenue. Until about ten years ago the Inland Revenue tax was £2 2*s*., and would in all probability have remained so had not Mr. John Manley Birch—one of the oldest established proprietors—sued the Crown for a rebate on the ground that as omnibuses came under the Hackney Carriage Act he could not be compelled to pay more than the hackney carriage tax of 15*s*. Mr. Birch's action was made a test case and was decided in his favour, one year's rebate being allowed.

When an omnibus is no longer fit for London work it is sold at auction, and becomes, eventually, a summer-house, a workmen's shed, a cricket club's dressing-room or refreshment bar. The London General Omnibus Company burns its old vehicles.

Until a few years ago it was a common thing for old London omnibuses to be purchased by colonial and provincial proprietors, and a "Kilburn" would be found at work at Liverpool, a "Camden Town" at Clacton-on-Sea, and a "Hammersmith" or "Bayswater" in New Zealand. But municipal authorities have, in most places, decided that an omnibus which is unfit to be at work in London must be regarded as unworthy to ply in their districts, and consequently the value of old omnibuses has fallen considerably.

English-built omnibuses are acknowledged to be the best obtainable, and Mr. Christopher Dodson, the well-known London coach-builder, supplies many of the leading continental proprietors. Mr. Dodson has recently invented a new staircase, which is more convenient for passengers, and reduces considerably the risk of accidents. It is already in use on some of the Road Car Company's Putney and Brondesbury omnibuses.

The nightly washing of omnibuses is an important matter, and the person who looks into an omnibus yard during the day would be surprised at its changed appearance if he were to see it late at night. About 10 o'clock the first omnibus arrives in the yard. On its way from the finishing point the conductor, lamp in hand, has searched the seats and floor of his omnibus, and found, perhaps, a stray penny. If he discovers a parcel, a purse, or anything of any value, he trudges off with it to the nearest police-station, bearing no grudge against the careless passenger who has made his walk necessary, for he knows that he will be rewarded, no matter whether the article is claimed or not. When the article is not claimed, he receives, eventually, a proportion of its value. If his search has proved fruitless, he and the coachman leave their omnibus as soon as it is in the yard, and depart for home, or the nearest public-house. But before they have quitted the yard the night men or "washers" have taken out the horses and led them into the stable. Sometimes they take them upstairs to bed. Then the washers unharness them and hang up the harness in the gangway. The collars, however, are hung under the number plates, for it is very necessary that every horse should have his own collar. The horses are then groomed, provided with food and water and secured for the night.

The washers are now ready for the next 'bus, which has probably by this time entered the yard. From midnight until nearly one o'clock 'bus follows 'bus in quick succession. Each has its appointed position in the yard, so that there shall be no hitch in its getting out at the proper time in the morning. When the last omnibus has entered, the stable-gates are locked and the men sit down to their supper. It is a lively meal, and if the day has been a dry one and the 'buses are not very dirty, they linger over it. If, however, there has been much rain, they hurry through it, for a wet day means very hard work for them. The 'buses have to be swept and swabbed, the wheels, the body, and the windows have to be cleaned, the brass work polished, the cushions brushed, and the aprons shaken and sponged. For some hours the yard is full of noise and bustle.

At five o'clock the coachbuilder's men arrive to test the wheels and thoroughly overhaul each omnibus, and in the event of their discovering any defect they repair it immediately. The coachbuilder's men are followed by the veterinary surgeon, who examines the horses; and if he thinks that any of them should have a rest he gives instructions to that effect to the foreman.

About seven o'clock the coachman and conductor of the omnibus which came in first on the previous night arrive, the former carrying his whip and rug, the latter with his little tin box—which contains his bell-punch and tickets—under his arm. In a few minutes the 'bus leaves the yard for its starting point. 'Bus after 'bus now passes out, and by ten o'clock the yard has a deserted appearance, fowls and geese being almost in sole possession, until the first change of horses is made.

## CHAPTER XII

Pirate Omnibuses—Their History and Tricks.

PIRATE omnibusmen—the pests of the streets of London—although not quite so numerous as once they were, continue, practically unchecked, to defraud ladies, children, foreigners and other unsuspecting persons whom they succeed in enticing into their travelling plunder-traps. The disreputable doings of these rascals have been the cause of a very large proportion of the complaints which have been made against omnibuses during the last seventy years.

One of the secrets of Shillibeer's early success was the care which he took to impress upon every man he employed the importance of politeness towards all passengers, and the seriousness with which he regarded any breach of that rule. But, in 1839, it was noticed that this high standard of politeness was not maintained by two or three conductors of the new omnibuses running from

Paddington to the Bank, *viâ* Oxford Street. They overcharged passengers, and met any protests with a torrent of abuse. Frequently, when females only were in the omnibus, they brought their journey to an end before they reached their advertised destination, compelling the passengers to walk a considerable distance after paying their fares. Shillibeer was inundated with complaints, and at once took steps to make it known that the omnibuses referred to were not his property, although they bore his name and were painted and lettered in imitation of his vehicles. These were the first pirate omnibuses. To let the public know which really were his vehicles, Shillibeer at once had painted on them "Shillibeer's Original Omnibus." In a few days the same inscription appeared on some of the pirates with the word "not" preceding it in very small letters.

When Shillibeer started his ill-fated Greenwich omnibuses the pirates followed in his wake, and soon made their presence known by their impudent cheating and bullying of passengers. One night, in April, 1836, some people returning to London saw what they believed to be one of Shillibeer's omnibuses ready to start. They entered it and sat down to wait until it was full. Within a quarter of an hour all the seats were occupied. But even then the omnibus did not start, for the conductor, in the bullying manner of his class, demanded the fares before the journey began. The passengers, anxious to get home, produced their money and tendered the usual fare—a shilling each. With a volley of oaths the conductor declared that the fare that night was eighteenpence. The passengers refused to pay the extra sixpence and threatened to report the conductor to Shillibeer for extortion and foul language, if he did not start the omnibus at once.

"Right away, Charlie," the conductor shouted; but there was something in the way he uttered those three words which gave the coachman the tip what to do, for he drove off immediately, not towards London, but down a back street to a deserted part of Greenwich, where he pulled up.

Again the conductor demanded eighteenpence from each person, and some were disposed to pay it; but the people who were the first to enter the omnibus declined most emphatically to submit to the extortion, and prevailed upon their fellow-passengers to be equally firm. Soon some of them wished that they had not been so firm, for when the conductor found that he could not obtain more than the proper fare he bawled out, "It's no good, Charlie. Let 'em walk to London."

The coachman got down from his box, took out his horses and went off with them at a trot, the conductor following with the omnibus lamp in his hand. In great indignation the passengers quitted the dark omnibus and wended their way back to the main street, vowing to let Shillibeer have a full account of everything that had occurred. But when on the following day they called on Shillibeer in a body, and complained of the men's behaviour, they were met with the inquiry, "What was the number of the omnibus?"

"588," was the answer in chorus.

"Gentlemen, that is not one of my omnibuses," Shillibeer replied; but he experienced some difficulty in convincing the deputation that he spoke the truth. Some of his hearers were determined not to let the matter rest there, and when they had satisfied themselves that the omnibus in which they had had such an unpleasant experience was not a Shillibeer, they published abroad, on their own responsibility, that omnibus No. 588 was a pirate. Their caution against that particular omnibus brought forth a large number of warnings against other pirates, and the nefarious practices of the objectionable vehicles being proved beyond all doubt, the Government passed a second Omnibus Bill, compelling drivers and conductors to be licensed. But legislation did not succeed in checking to any great extent the fraudulent doings of the pirates.

The first real check they received came, a few years later, from the proprietors of respectably-conducted omnibuses, whose vehicles were imitated just as Shillibeer's had been. These proprietors were now in a position to assert themselves, having just formed themselves into Associations. The associated proprietors started a crusade against pirates, and subjected them daily to a rigorous course of "nursing," which is not such a harmless performance as it sounds, consisting as it does of two omnibuses working together to prevent a third from making a profitable journey. One of the Association's omnibuses would keep just in front of the pirate, and the other close behind it, with the result that, there being three omnibuses where one would have been sufficient, none of them earned enough to pay expenses. The Associations were quite prepared to lose money, and when the pirates understood this they changed their tactics quickly. Whenever a pirate found it was going to be "nursed," it would turn off the main road and wander about the back streets until its "nurses" had gone on. Then it would make another start in a clear road. To render that proceeding profitless, the Associations told off an omnibus to follow each pirate wherever it went. The result was that two omnibuses, sometimes empty, sometimes carrying mixed loads of amused, frightened, and indignant passengers, were frequently to be seen careering along quiet back streets with scarcely a yard dividing them. This state of things had existed for a few weeks, when a pirate owner heard something which caused him considerable uneasiness, and prompted him to keep a close watch on his men. The following morning he witnessed his omnibus begin its daily struggle, and eventually disappear down a side street closely followed by its "nurse." He then walked to a quiet little inn some three miles away, arriving there in time to discover the rival 'busmen enjoying themselves at a friendly game of skittles, while their omnibuses stood empty in the road.

On one occasion a pirate scored off its opponents in a novel way. Having made several ineffectual attempts to obtain passengers, it started off into the country, followed by its "nurse." When they had travelled some miles the driver of the respectable omnibus was surprised by seeing a gate suddenly closed in front of his horses, preventing him from following the pirate. At the same moment a gate clanged behind him, and, looking round, he discovered that he had been trapped. He had, in fact, followed the pirate on to its proprietor's little farm. "'Ere you are, and 'ere you'll stay," the irate owner declared, with many oaths; while the pirate driver, with taunting shouts of laughter, whipped up his horses and started back to town. The farmer omnibus-proprietor made no attempt to detain the Association's men, but its omnibus and horses he held prisoners until the following morning, releasing them one hour after his own omnibus had started out.

In 1855 the London General Omnibus Company came into existence, and had been established but a very short time when the pirates were repainted and lettered in close imitation of its omnibuses. They have continued to imitate them, but not always with impunity, ever since, and many thousands of people have entered pirates firmly believing they were the Company's vehicles. Nine or ten years ago the pirates' audacity in imitating the general appearance of the London General omnibuses was at its height, and certainly the imitations of their decoration and lettering were excellent enough to deceive all but the very wary. Unable to paint "London General Omnibus Company, Limited," on their panels, they had in its place some inscription which might, at a glance, be taken for it. The favourite one was "London General Post Office, Lothbury."

There are also many pirates who lure passengers into their omnibuses by having them painted to resemble the London Road Car Company's vehicles.

The pirate is naturally of a roving disposition, and by no means restricts itself to one route: a "Kilburn" may be seen at Blackwall, or a "Bayswater" at Bethnal Green. But Oxford Circus is the place best loved by pirates, and any day of the week they can be seen walking to and fro, ready to begin their journey as soon as they see a number of ladies waiting on the pavement.

During shopping hours pirates are continually running to and from Oxford Circus, but it is interesting to notice that the name of their destination very rarely appears on them. "Regent Circus" is put up instead, and the public having doubts as to which really is Regent Circus, the pirates obtain passengers for both Oxford Circus and Piccadilly Circus, and turn them out at whichever they like. It is a great pity that the local authorities do not have the name Regent Circus, which is still displayed at Oxford Circus, removed, for it affords the pirate-omnibus men an excuse for painting on their vehicles a destination which is misleading. The Oxford Street shopkeepers should, in the interests of their customers, see to this, and, remembering that the police stated in court a few years ago that one, at least, of the pirate omnibuses which frequented Oxford Circus was worked in collusion with pickpockets, insist upon a closer watch being kept on the pests.

In the summer many pirates run to Kew Gardens on Sundays, and the exorbitant fares they charge—they collect them on alighting—spoil the day's pleasure of many a poorly-paid clerk. Some pirates run on to Hampton Court, and a trick of theirs on these occasions should always be borne in mind. When one of them gets well beyond Richmond, and all fares have been paid—they collect them on these vehicles soon after crossing Richmond Bridge—a horse is supposed to fall lame, and the coachman declares, with many expressions of regret, that he cannot go any further. The passengers are wondering what they shall do, when another pirate omnibus comes along. The driver of the first omnibus calls out to the driver of the second, "You'll take these ladies and gentlemen on for me, won't you, Jack?" Jack answers in the affirmative, and the passengers change into his omnibus, quite believing that it belongs to the same proprietor as the other. It generally does, but, nevertheless, when they have driven on another mile or two, the conductor comes round for fares, and, in spite of indignant protests, they have to pay. By that time the first omnibus is back at Richmond picking up fares for London. In the evening it will make a shorter journey on a different road.

Two or three bullies always ride on the long-distance pirate omnibuses, and their fellow-travellers, as a rule, have not the slightest suspicion that they are not ordinary passengers. Of course they pay the second fare without a murmur, and if any other passenger does not follow their example they express great astonishment that any one could be so mean as to attempt to *swindle* a poor 'bus conductor. Generally that contemptuous speech has the desired effect—the passenger submits to being cheated. But sometimes a man is smart enough to guess that the indignant passengers are friends of the conductor, and is rash enough to say so. If he looks the kind of man that can be frightened, the bullies discard their *rôle* of being disinterested passengers, and join the conductor in swearing at him and threatening him alternately with personal violence and the police. Frequently those threats cause the passenger and his friends to pay up without any further complaints; but sometimes the bullies meet with a surprise—the passengers threaten them. Now, the pirate conductor, although frequently a big beery-faced fellow, is usually a cowardly cur, and his dislike of a thrashing is exceeded only by his abhorrence of police courts and magistrates. Therefore he changes his tone, and requests the passengers to get out if they will not pay; and naturally they oblige him.

Decoy women are another speciality of pirate omnibuses starting for a long Sunday run into the country. Showily dressed, these women take their seats on top of the omnibus at its starting place with the idea of giving an air of respectability to the vehicle. If the omnibus fills up quickly they pretend to remember that they have left something at home—their money perhaps—and must of course go back for it; but, if it does not fill, they go for the ride.

A few pirates cater on Sunday mornings for the lowest of the lower classes by running a few miles out to some suburban public-house. There are no restrictions as to behaviour in these omnibuses. A passenger may smoke, spit and swear, inside or out, to his heart's content. Moreover, he may take in with him dogs, ferrets, rats, bird-cages and beer. The conductor smokes a clay pipe and talks, with the air of an authority, of sporting matters. Several passengers offer him drinks from their private bottles. He accepts them all, and yet never forgets to collect the fares inside before going on top.

A few years ago I gave the following answer, to the oft-repeated question, "How can you tell a pirate?" "No pirates issue tickets; therefore, before entering an omnibus, see if the conductor has a ticket-punch or roll of tickets. If he has you may enter his 'bus assured that it belongs to one of the London Companies or Associations. It is not, however, suggested that *every* omnibus which does not issue tickets is a pirate, for Messrs. Balls Brothers' Brixton omnibuses,* and a few others, are exceptions."

Unfortunately, the pirate conductors read my advice, and some of them quickly rendered it nugatory by wearing punches and holding packets of tickets in their hands so that every one might see them. The punches differed, however, in appearance from those used by the Companies and Associations.

A similar dodge was very common among pirates immediately after the great strike, when the ticket system was in its infancy and con-

* Messrs. Balls Brothers adopted the ticket system on August 26, 1901.

ductors of the various companies carried rolls of paper tickets. The pirate conductors provided themselves with ticket-rolls, but once passengers were safe in their omnibuses they never troubled to tear off and issue the tickets. One old lady, deceived by a pirate's appearance, entered it, in the belief that it was one of the London General's omnibuses, and ensconced herself comfortably in the far corner. After a time the conductor entered, collected her fare and returned to the door without giving her a ticket. For a few moments the old lady eyed him sorrowfully. Then she said in a tone of gentle reproof, "Conductor, you haven't given me a ticket."

"Want a ticket, lady?" the conductor replied cheerfully. "'Ere you are, then; take a bloomin' yard of 'em," and tearing off a long string of tickets dropped it in coils in the astonished passenger's lap.

But the favourite reply of pirate conductors when asked for a ticket is, "We don't have to give tickets. We're honest men on these 'buses."

In conclusion, I would point out that the London General, the Road Car, and the other Companies and Associations described in Chapter

VI., between them cover the whole of London, and there is, therefore, not the slightest necessity for any one to enter a pirate. All the would-be passenger has to do is to refrain from placing the slightest reliance on the colour of the omnibus, but to see that it bears on the panels the name of one of the Companies or Associations which I have mentioned.

Visitors to London should take note of the fact that Christmas Eve is the day on which pirates reap a big harvest.

# PART II

## *CABS*

# CHAPTER I

The introduction of hackney-coaches—"The world run on wheels"—The first hackney-coach stand and the oldest cab rank in England—Sedan chairs introduced—Charles I. and Charles II. prohibit hackney-coaches—Hackney-coaches and the Plague—William Congreve—Threatened strike of hackney-coachmen—Hackney-chariots introduced—Prince of Wales drives a hackney-coach—Licences—Funeral coaches ply for hire in the streets—A pedometer for hackney-coaches suggested—Dickens on hackney-coaches—Origin of the word "hackney."

There are, at the present day, many old people who remember and speak with affection of the old hackney-coach. They admit that it was a lumbering thing, and that the horses were generally sorry specimens fully qualified for the knacker's yard; but they add, emphatically, that no vehicles now plying for hire in the streets of London can compare with it for cosiness and comfort. It was furnished luxuriously, and was as comfortable as a hammock, even when travelling on roads that would shake a modern cab to pieces before it had journeyed half a mile.

Hackney-coaches were established in London early in the seventeenth century, and soon became so well patronised that, in 1623, the Thames watermen, who had long enjoyed the monopoly of carrying the public, became alarmed and complained loudly that they were being ruined. Apparently they wished the hackney-coaches to be suppressed, but the new vehicles were far too popular to be treated in that fashion.

John Taylor, the waterman-poet, bewailed their introduction in a pamphlet entitled, "The world run on wheels." He did not denounce private coaches, his anger being aroused "only against the caterpillar swarm of hirelings. They have undone my poor trade whereof I am a member: and though I look for no reformation yet I expect the benefit of an old proverb, 'Give the losers leave to speak.' . . . This infernal swarm of trade-spellers have so overrun the land that we can get no living upon the water; for I dare truly affirm that in every day in any term, especially if the Court be at Whitehall, they do rob us of our livings and carry 500 fares daily from us."

"I have heard," he continued, "of a gentlewoman who sent her man to Smithfield from

Charing Cross to hire a coach to carry her to Whitehall; another did the like from Ludgate Hill to be carried to see a play at Blackfriars."

One is tempted to believe that Taylor was exaggerating in the hope of checking by ridicule the growing fashion for hackney-coach riding.

"It is," he declared in the same pamphlet, "a most uneasy kind of passage in coaches on the paved streets of London, wherein men and women are so tost, tumbled, jumbled, rumbled, and crossing of kennels, dunghills, and uneven ways."

In spite of the protests of the Thames watermen and their friends, hackney-coaches grew in popular favour. Until 1634, they stood for hire in the yards of the principal inns, but in that year Captain Baily, a retired mariner, made an experiment. He had four superior coaches built, and stationed them for hire at the Maypole in the Strand, where St. Mary's Church now stands. The cab rank at the side of St. Mary's Church is, therefore, the oldest in England. Baily's drivers, attired in livery, were instructed as to the charges they should make for driving people to various parts of the town. So successful was this venture that other hackney-coachmen began to take up their stand at the same place and carry passengers at Captain Baily's rates. Soon the rank became so crowded that the practice of driving slowly along the streets plying for hire was begun by hackney-coachmen who could not find room for their vehicles at the stand.

Garrard mentions this innovation in a letter to Lord Strafford :—

"I cannot omit to mention any new thing that comes up amongst us, though never so trivial : here is one Captain Baily, he hath been a sea-captain, but now lives on the land, about this city, where he tries experiments. He hath erected, according to his ability, some four hackney-coaches, put his men in livery, and appointed them to stand at the Maypole in the Strand, giving them instructions at what rates to carry men into several parts of the town, where all day they may be had. Other hackney-men seeing this way, they flocked to the same place, and perform their journeys at the same rate; so that sometimes there are twenty of them together, which disperse up and down, that they and others are to be had everywhere, as watermen are to be had by the waterside. Everybody is much pleased with it; for, whereas, before, coaches could not be had but at greater rates, now a man may have one much cheaper."

Charles I. did not, however, regard hackney-coaches with favour, and endeavoured to check Captain Baily's enterprise by granting to Sir Sanders Duncomb the sole right to let on hire sedan chairs, which, until then, were unknown in England. The patent stated:—

"Whereas the streets of our cities of London and Westminster and their suburbs are of late so much encumbered with the unnecessary multitude of coaches, that many of our subjects are thereby exposed to great danger and the necessary use of carts and carriages for provisions much hindered: and Sir Sanders Duncomb's petition representing that in many parts beyond sea, people are much carried in chairs that are covered, whereby few coaches are used among them: wherefore we have granted to him the sole privilege to use, let, or hire a number of the said covered chairs for fourteen years."

Sedan chairs did not prove to be formidable rivals to the hackney-coaches, but they added considerably to the congestion of the streets. For this congestion the hackney-coaches were blamed, and on January 19, 1635, a proclamation was made "to restrain the multitude and promiscuous use of coaches about London and Westminster."

The proclamation was to the effect that "hackney-coaches were not only a great disturbance to his Majesty, his dearest consort the Queen, the nobility and others of place and degree in their passage through the streets; but the streets themselves were so pestered and the pavements so broken up, that the common passage is thereby hindered and made dangerous; and the prices of hay, provender, etc., thereby made exceeding dear. Wherefore we expressly command and forbid that no hackney-coaches or hired carriages be used or suffered in London, Westminster, or the suburbs thereof, except they be to travel at least three miles out of the same. And also that no person shall go in a coach to the said streets except the owner of the coach shall constantly keep up four able horses for our service when required."

This proclamation was either withdrawn or ignored, for in the following year there were many hackney-coaches plying for hire in London and

Westminster, and the rivalry between hackney-coachmen and sedan-chairmen was humorously depicted in a pamphlet entitled, "Coach and Sedan pleasantly disputing for place and precedence."

In 1654, Parliament limited the number of hackney-coaches in London and Westminster to three hundred, with two horses apiece. It was also ordained that the government and regulation of hackney-coaches should be in the hands of the Court of Aldermen, and for the expense of regulating them, a tax of twenty shillings a year was placed on every vehicle.

A few months after the Restoration hackney-coaches were forbidden, by a proclamation dated October 18, 1660, to ply for hire in the streets. But that this edict was evaded we have the authority of the delightful Samuel Pepys. Writing under the date of November 7 he states:—

"Notwithstanding that this was the first day of the king's proclamation against hackney coaches coming into the streets to stand to be hired, yet I got one to carry me home."

In 1661 they numbered four hundred. They were small, narrow vehicles, drawn by two horses, on one of which sat the driver, wearing spurs and carrying a short whip. It was found, however, that they were very destructive to the paving-stones, and a tax of £5 a year was therefore placed on all hackney-coaches, the money thus obtained being expended on the repairing and cleansing of the roads.

During the Plague infected persons were frequently conveyed to the Pest-houses in hackney-coaches. Defoe mentions this in his "Journal of the Plague Year." In the "Orders conceived and published by the Lord Mayor and Alderman of the City of London, concerning the infection of the plague, 1665," appears the following order:—"That care be taken of hackney-coachmen, that they may not (as some of them have been observed to do), after carrying of infected persons to the Pest-house, and other places, be admitted to common use, till their coaches be well aired, and have stood unemployed by the space of five or six days after such service."

After the Great Fire, when the streets were widened, more commodious vehicles came into use, the majority being disused family coaches which had been sold cheaply by the nobility and gentry.

Their coats of arms were not removed from the panels, and such coaches as bore the heraldic devices of the most aristocratic houses invariably received the greatest patronage. In 1694 some masked women hired a coach decorated with a well-known coat of arms, and went for a drive in Hyde Park. It is recorded that their behaviour

HACKNEY-COACH. ABOUT 1680.

was disgraceful, and that they deliberately insulted some very distinguished people who were riding in their private coaches. What they said or did will never be known, but from that day hackney-coaches were prohibited from entering Hyde Park. In the same year a tax of £4 per annum was placed on hackney-coaches, and the cost of a licence became £50. The licence held good for twenty-one years. The same Act of Parliament ordained that the number of hackney-coaches should not exceed seven hundred.

In the early part of the following year William Congreve, the poet, was appointed a Commissioner for Licensing Hackney-Coaches, at the moderate salary of £100 a year, and retained the position until October, 1707. Possibly the Hackney-Coach Licence Office was not loved by Congreve, and when he left it each day he banished all thought of it until the morrow. The idea of writing anything about it, in all probability never occurred to him. "Who would be interested in hearing anything concerning that dull, wearisome office?" he might have asked had any one made the suggestion, and possibly very few people of that day would have troubled to read anything on the subject. But to us an account of his duties, with some description of the hackney-coach proprietors and drivers with whom he came into contact daily, would be of more than ordinary interest.

Early in the eighteenth century several thieves, not sufficiently daring to attack stage-coaches, cut through the backs of hackney-coaches, snatched off the passengers' wigs and decamped with them.

In 1711 Parliament once more altered the regulations concerning hackney-coaches. The annual tax of £4 was changed to a weekly one of five shillings, and the number of licences was increased to eight hundred. The fares which the hackney-coachmen were authorised to charge were fixed at a shilling for one mile and a half, eighteenpence for two miles, and sixpence for every additional mile or portion of a mile.

Under the new regulations hackney-coaches enjoyed almost unbroken prosperity for over fifty years, and, on the whole, gave satisfaction to the public. There was, however, one occasion on which they became very unpopular. A few days prior to the coronation of George III., the hackney-coach and the sedan-chair men agreed that unless they were allowed to charge greatly increased prices on Coronation day, they would refuse to take out their coaches and chairs. This decision created considerable indignation among people who wished to ride but did not possess vehicles of their own, and the Lords of the Privy Council issued a proclamation that all hackney-coachmen and sedan-chairmen were to be out with their coaches and chairs at four o'clock in the morning of Coronation day; they were, moreover, warned that if they demanded more than the ordinary fares, or failed to perform their duties properly, they would be punished with the utmost severity. This proclamation did not have the desired effect. The men decided to defy the authorities, and would certainly have done so had not a well-known sedan-chair maker advised them to go to work and trust to the generosity of the public. He assured them that he had been told by numerous regular users of hackney-coaches and sedan-chairs that they were perfectly willing to pay, unasked, considerably more than the legal fares. So the men went to work, and the majority reaped a splendid harvest. Some people declined to pay more than the usual fare, but they were not sufficiently numerous to prevent the day being a memorable one for hackney-coachmen.

In 1768 there were a thousand hackney-coaches licensed to stand for hire in the streets. Of these only 175 were allowed to ply for hire on Sundays.

By an Act of George III. a commission was formed for the management of hackney-coaches and the receipt of duties. Stands were appointed in various parts of London, and coachmen were forbidden to wait for hire at any other places. Men were also licensed to water the horses at the various stands. These men were known as "watermen," "caddies" or "cads," and wore, slung round their necks, a brass label bearing a number. Besides watering the horses they looked after them while the coachmen drank in the tap-room or slept on their boxes, and, also, opened the coach doors and lowered the steps for hirers. Every coachman before driving off a rank paid the waterman one halfpenny.

One clause of this Act appears, nowadays, very snobbish. It made a hackney-coachman liable to a penalty of £5 for "not giving way to persons of quality and gentlemen's coaches."

As time went on, hackney-coaches continued to increase in number, but were never allowed to become sufficiently numerous to make competition very keen. At the end of the eighteenth century they were most luxurious. The majority originally cost some £700 or £800 each, and were purchased from the brokers by hackney-coach proprietors at a trifle above breaking-up prices, varying, according to the condition of the vehicles, from £25 to £50. To illustrate their commodiousness, a well-known coachbuilder, now dead, was fond of telling the following story. When he was a youngster, he had a difference with

HACKNEY-COACH. ABOUT 1800.

another boy in Old Palace Yard and proceeded to settle it in the time-honoured British fashion, much to the delight of the hackney-coachmen on the rank. To their intense disgust, however, an energetic member of the newly-established police force appeared on the scene and stopped the fight. Only for a time though, for one of the men bundled the boys into his own hackney-coach and told them to fight it out there. They did; the sport-loving, many-caped coachmen crowding round and watching them through the windows.

Early in the nineteenth century a more lightly built hackney-coach, named a "chariot," which was introduced many years previously, became popular. It carried two inside passengers and had room for a third on the box seat. The driver usually rode on the near-side horse, but some men drove from the box. In 1814 there were two hundred licensed chariots in London, and for a few years the number increased rapidly. Some of the chariots licensed in 1815 had accommodation for three inside passengers.

With the young bloods of the day hackney-coachmen were great favourites, chiefly because they looked on with marked approval while their fares wrenched off a knocker, assaulted a policeman, or kissed a pretty girl. Moreover, their memory was most defective when necessary.

One night a hackney-coachman was called to the

British Coffee House in Cockspur Street to take up the Prince of Wales, afterwards George IV. The First Gentleman of Europe was in one of his lively moods and commanded the coachman to get down and let him drive. The astonished driver began to make excuses, but the Prince cut them short by seizing the man and pitching him bodily through the open window into the coach. Then, quickly mounting the box, he drove off at an exciting speed. Questioned later as to how His Royal Highness acquitted himself, the hackney-coachman replied, "The Prince isn't such a bad driver. Indeed, he drove very well for a prince; but he didn't take the corners and crossings careful enough for a regular jarvey."

Hackney-coachmen prided themselves on being dashing fellows, and no self-respecting member of the profession was ever without at least one adoring lady-love. Just as nowadays servant-girls of all ages, sizes and shapes, are consumed with one great desire—to have a soldier to "walk out with," so the girls of that class sixty to a hundred years ago considered it the summit of happiness to be seen leaning on the arm of a hackney-coachman. As a rule, the hackney-coachman had plenty of girls to choose from, and, that being the case, he was naturally rather particular about whom he selected for the honour of being allowed to cook his meals for the remainder of his life.

Hackney-coachmen were not licensed. Any man might drive a hackney-coach, but the proprietor, himself licensed, was held responsible for the actions of his men. No person could obtain a licence to possess a hackney-coach unless he was recommended by a peer, a Member of Parliament, or some other influential being; consequently, a large number of hackney-coach proprietors were men who had been gentlemen's servants. And in the interests of these men the hackney-coach business was not allowed to become overcrowded. The number of licence-plates issued never exceeded one thousand, in spite of the fact that, in the early part of last century, the public were complaining constantly that there were not sufficient hackney-coaches plying for hire.

The hackney-coach fares were, at this period, one shilling a mile, and sixpence extra for every additional half-mile or part of half a mile. The waiting fare was three shillings an hour for the first three hours, and two shillings for every additional hour or part of an hour. For the licence-plate affixed to the vehicle the proprietor had to pay ten shillings a week.

In compliance with a legal requirement every driver was paid a small salary, generally nine shillings a week, but that formed a very insignificant portion of his income, for, like the cabman of to-day, he could keep all that he earned beyond the hire money due to the proprietor.

Mourning coaches, commonly called "black coaches," bore licence-plates, and when not engaged at funerals plied for hire in the streets. The number of these vehicles was limited, but every undertaker kept in reserve many for which he had no licences, as, in the event of requiring more coaches for a funeral than he possessed licences, he had the power to go to any rank and remove from the hackney-coaches standing there as many licence-plates as he wanted. These plates he would affix to his unlicensed vehicles, and for the loan of each would have to pay the hackney-coachman waiting fare.

In the first quarter of the last century, hackney-coach proprietors were blackmailed systematically by two or three men who made a comfortable living as common informers. One of these fellows would stroll into a hackney-coach yard, greet the proprietor in a very friendly way and have a chat with him on any topic of the day. The conversation always ended, however, in one way—with a request by the informer that the proprietor would lend him half a sovereign. In most cases the proprietor, knowing who the man was, complied with the request at once, and nothing more would be seen of the borrower for a month or two. But if the proprietor refused the "loan," he received, in the course of a day or two, a summons for some irregularity in connection with his drivers, his vehicles, or his horses. The informer received one-half of every fine that was imposed. These blackmailers flourished long after the introduction of cabs, and when at last their nefarious business was stopped, they were succeeded by blackmailers of another class. Strange as it may seem, forty years ago it was a common thing for the proprietors of a large number of horses to submit to being blackmailed by men whose duty it was to keep an eye on their studs.

In 1822, an order was issued compelling

hackney-coachmen to take to the office of the Registrar of Licences all articles found in their vehicles. The losers, on applying at the office, had their property restored to them, upon payment of a small fee to be given to the coachman. It is said, however, that valuable articles lost in hackney-coaches were very rarely recovered; it was only minor things that were taken to the office. Hackney-coachmen had, some years previously, been considered an honest set of men, but they had sadly deteriorated, as had also their vehicles. A correspondent of the *London Magazine*, signing himself "Jehu," gave, in 1825, the following description of a hackney-coach:—

"A hackney-coach—fogh! Who can be a gentleman and visit in a hackney-coach? Who can, indeed? to predicate nothing of stinking wet straw and broken windows, and cushions on which the last dandy has cleaned his shoes, and of the last fever it has carried to Guy's, or the last load of convicts transported to the hulks."

He was also troubled about the hackney-coachmen's extortion, and suggested this method of checking it. "Is there any valid reason why a hackney-coach should not have a pedometer visible to the unfortunate freight? to be noted on entering, to be noted on exiting, as effectual against fraudulent space as a watch is against fraudulent time, with shillings on the dial plate where there are hours; and where there are minutes, sixpences. It would not cost £2, it would save endless altercations, it would save typographying a table of hackney-coach fares, it would save a man's money and temper, and go far towards saving the souls of hackney-coachmen born, or to be born — and the trouble of the commissioners. Our invention is the best of all possible inventions, and therefore it will not be adopted."

"Jehu" did not make a mistake—his suggestion was not adopted, and hackney-coachmen, soured by the rivalry of the newly introduced omnibuses and cabs, became more extortionate and abusive than ever they had been.

A few proprietors, believing that the new vehicles were doomed to failure, kept their hackney-coaches in good repair and made it a rule to have respectable men for drivers, but these clean coaches were not numerous enough to prevent hackney-coaches as a body from being termed dirty and disreputable. In "Sketches by Boz," Dickens gives the following description of a hackney-coach of the early thirties :—

"There is a hackney-coach stand under the very window at which we are writing; there is only one coach on it now, but it is a fair specimen of the class of vehicles to which we have alluded—a great, lumbering, square concern of a dingy yellow colour (like a bilious brunette), with very small glasses, but very large frames; the panels are ornamented with a faded coat of arms, in shape something like a dissected bat, the axletree is red, and the majority of the wheels are green. The box is partially covered by an old great-coat, with a multiplicity of capes, and some extraordinary-looking clothes; and the straw, with which the canvas cushion is stuffed, is sticking up in several places, as if in rivalry with the hay which is peering through the chinks in the boot. The horses, with drooping heads, and each with a mane and tail as scanty and straggling as those of a worn-out rocking-horse, are standing patiently on some damp straw, occasionally wincing and rattling the harness; and, now and then, one of them lifts his mouth to the ear of his companion, as if he were saying, in a whisper, that he should like to assassinate the coachman. The coachman himself is in the watering-house; and the waterman, with his hands forced into his pockets as far as they can possibly go, is dancing the 'double shuffle' in front of the pump, to keep his feet warm."

A writer in the *Monthly Magazine* gives a less graphic but more denunciatory account of the hackney-coaches of that period.

"Nothing in nature or art can be so abominable as those vehicles at this hour. We are quite satisfied that, except an Englishman, who will endure anything, no native of any climate under the sky would endure a London hackney-coach; that an Ashantee gentleman would scoff at it; and that an aboriginal of New South Wales would refuse to be inhumed within its shattered and infinite squalidness. It is true that the vehicle has its merits, if variety of uses can establish them. The hackney-coach conveys alike the living and the dead. It carries the dying man to the hospital, and when doctors and tax-gatherers can tantalize no more, it carries him to Surgeons' Hall and qualifies him to assist the 'march of mind' by the section of body. If the midnight thief finds his plunder too ponderous for his hands, the hackney-coach offers its services, and is one of the most expert conveyances. Its other employments are many, and equally meritorious, and doubtless society would find a vacuum in its loss. Yet we cordially wish that the Maberley brain were set at work upon this subject, and some substitute contrived."

Hackney-coaches died hard. In 1841, there were four hundred plying for hire, but before the Great Exhibition of 1851, nearly all the proprietors who possessed sufficient capital had sold their hackney-coaches at breaking-up prices, and started cabs. Nevertheless, as late as 1858, hackney-coaches were to be seen occasionally in the streets.

The origin of the word "hackney" cannot be decided. In all probability it was derived from the old French word "*hacquenèe*," which was applied to horses—and sometimes coaches—let on hire. The claim that Hackney was the first place where coaches could be hired, and gave its name to the vehicles, does not bear investigation.

## CHAPTER II

Cabs introduced into England—Restrictions placed upon them—A comical-looking cab—Dickens on cabs—Hackney-coachmen wish to become cabmen—The cab business a monopoly—Restrictions are removed—*The Cab* paper—The Boulnois cab invented—The "minibus"—The "duobus"—Bilking—A peer's joke.

NEARLY one hundred years have elapsed since Londoners, growing dissatisfied with the lumbering hackney-coaches plying for hire in the metropolis, began to advocate the introduction of the *cabriolet de place*, which for some considerable time had been exceedingly popular in Paris. Unfortunately, the hackney-coach proprietors had been granted the sole right of carrying people within the bills of mortality—an area which contained the most thickly populated parts of London and nearly all the places of entertainment—and naturally they protested strongly against the introduction of what might prove to be formidable rivals to their slow-travelling vehicles. But in 1805 cabriolet promoters received a slight encouragement, Messrs. Bradshaw and Rotch—the latter a member of Parliament—obtaining licences for nine of their vehicles on the condition that they never entered within the bills of mortality. In appearance the cabriolet resembled the modern gig, and carried two people only, the driver sitting side by side with his fare. In consequence of the limited area in which they were allowed to ply for hire, the new vehicles attracted little attention, but, on April 23, 1823, twelve fully-licensed cabriolets, built by Mr. David Davies, were placed on the streets. They were announced as being "introduced to the public in honour of his Majesty's birthday." These cabriolets were a decided improvement upon their predecessors, as each one had accommodation for two passengers. The driver, whose proximity to his fare had proved to be the reverse of a pleasure to riders, was relegated to a comical-looking seat built out on the off side, between the body of the vehicle and the wheel. The hood strongly resembled a coffin standing on end, and earned for the vehicle the nickname of "coffin-cab." The fore part of the hood could be lowered as required, and there was a curtain which could be drawn across to shield the rider from

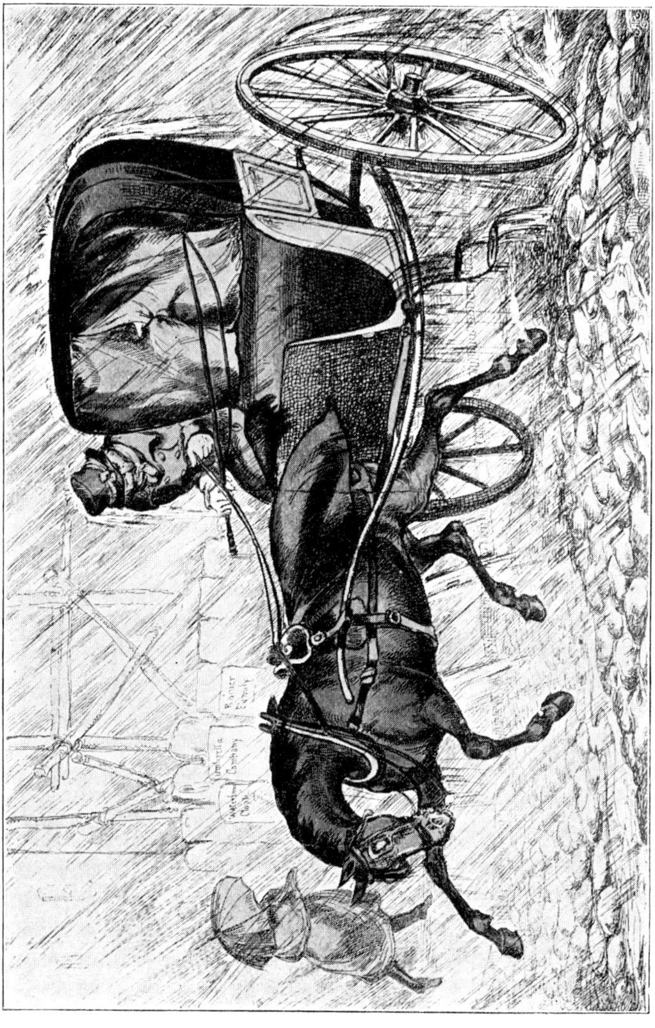

LONDON CAB OF 1823, WITH CURTAIN DRAWN.

wind or rain. The fare was eightpence a mile and fourpence for every additional half-mile or part of half a mile. Each vehicle carried, in a leather pocket made for the purpose, a book of fares for the convenience of hirers.

In a short time cabriolets became very popular, and a topical song of the period contains the following verse :—

> "In days of old when folks got tired,
> A hackney coach or a chariot was hired;
> But now along the streets they roll ye
> In a *shay* with a cover called a cabrioly."

The French name of the vehicle was soon abbreviated to "cab," and, although the word was at first considered deplorably vulgar, convenience triumphed quickly over the objections of purists.

To be able to travel cheaply and quickly was a pleasing novelty to Londoners, but many of them lived to regret having trusted themselves in a cab, for the drivers, proud of being able to pass hackney and private coaches, were fond of showing their superior speed, and while doing so frequently ran against street posts or collided with other vehicles; and when either of these things happened, or the horse fell, the "fare" was usually pitched forward into the road. This danger, coupled with the difficulty of climbing into a cab, prevented old men and women from patronising the new vehicle. They remained satisfied with hackney-coaches, but young and middle-aged men—"dandies" and shopmen striving to imitate them—gloried in cabs, and many of them boasted of the number of times they had been thrown out of them.

Dickens on several occasions mentioned the cabs of this period. Describing, in "Sketches by Boz," morning in the streets of London, he wrote—

"Cabs, with trunks and band-boxes between the drivers' legs and outside the apron, rattle briskly up and down the streets on their way to the coach-offices or steam-packet wharfs; and the cab-drivers and hackney coachmen who are on the stand polish up the ornamental part of their dingy vehicles—the former wondering how people can prefer 'them wild beast cariwans of homnibuses to a riglar cab with a fast trotter,' and the latter admiring how people can trust their necks into one of 'them crazy cabs, when they can have a 'spectable 'ackney cotche with a pair of 'orses as von't run away with no vun;' a consolation unquestionably founded on fact, seeing that a hackney-coach horse never was known to run at all, ‘except,’ as the smart cabman in front of the rank observes, ‘except one, and *he* run back’ards.’ ’

THE “COFFIN-CAB.”

“Talk of cabs!” the great novelist wrote in

his article on Hackney-Coach Stands. "Cabs are all very well in cases of expedition, when it's a matter of neck or nothing, life or death, your temporary home or your long one. But, besides a cab's lacking that gravity of deportment which so peculiarly distinguishes a hackney-coach, let it never be forgotten that a cab is a thing of yesterday, and that he was never anything better. A hackney-cab has always been a hackney-cab, from his first entry into public life; whereas a hackney-coach is a remnant of past gentility, a victim to fashion, a hanger-on of an old English family, wearing their arms, and, in days of yore, escorted by men wearing their livery, stripped of his finery, and thrown upon the world, like a once smart footman when he is no longer sufficiently juvenile for his office, progressing lower and lower in the scale of four-wheeled degradation, until at last it comes to—*a stand!*"

The growing popularity of the cabs soon thoroughly alarmed the hackney-coachmen, who at first had jeered at the new vehicle and prophesied a short career for it. They endeavoured to get their licence-plates transferred to cabs, but were unsuccessful, for the cab proprietors of that period were men of good social position—some of them occupying Government appointments—and all the influence which they could command was exerted to keep the trade in their own hands. In spite of the protests of the hackney-coach proprietors this monopoly existed for nearly ten years, and many of the aristocratic cab owners amassed money rapidly. They did not believe in having a large number of cabs, even of their own, on the streets, and for some months there were only fifty. Afterwards the number was raised to one hundred, and in 1831, to one hundred and fifty. In Paris in the same year, there were nearly two thousand five hundred of them! In 1832, when the number of London cabs reached one hundred and sixty-five, the disgraceful monopoly was put an end to, and, all restrictions being removed, hackney-coach proprietors were at last enabled to transfer their licences from their coaches to cabs. In a few weeks there were several hundred cabs, and other two-wheel vehicles, plying for hire in the streets.

A paper called *The Cab* was started immediately, but the title was chosen simply to attract attention, as, although the publication bore on the front page a small and blurred illustration of a cab, its contents were literary odds and ends. In the "Answers to Correspondents" column, a cabman's MS. was declined with thanks. Its non-publication is to be regretted.

Some months later a new cab, invented and patented by Mr. William Boulnois, father of Mr. Edmund Boulnois, M.P., was placed on the streets. It was a two-wheeled closed vehicle, constructed to carry two passengers sitting face to face. The driver sat on a small and particularly unsafe seat on the top of it, and the door was at the back. It was, in fact, so much like the front of an omnibus that it was well known as "the omnibus slice." Its popular name was "the back-door cab." Superior people called it a "minibus." This cab was quickly followed by a very similar, although larger, vehicle invented by Mr. Harvey. It was called a "duobus," a name frequently applied to Mr. Boulnois's cab.

A young man of good family, who had squandered a fortune, conceived the idea of earning his living by driving a back-door cab of his own. His friends having supplied him with the necessary capital, he created a sensation by appearing one morning in the Haymarket driving a superbly fitted and splendidly horsed cab. The result of his first morning's work was very satisfactory, and the young cabman was in high spirits. But driving to the stables, his horse stumbled and fell, and, taken by surprise, the unfortunate young cabman was pitched head-first into the road, and killed on the spot.

BOULNOIS'S CAB.

But the driver's unsafe seat was not the only weak point about the back-door cab. The facilities it offered for alighting without paying, soon made "bilking" a popular amusement with a certain class of people.

A somewhat rackety young peer proved, for a wager, how easy it was to "bilk" a cabman. He hailed a cab outside his club and told the cabby to drive him to a certain address at Hammersmith.

Just before he arrived at his destination he got out unobserved, and from a distance watched cabby's surprise and wrath on discovering his vehicle to be empty. After a time the cabman started back for town, and the youthful lord, seizing his opportunity, re-entered the cab, and shouted almost immediately, in well-assumed anger, "Hi, you rascal! Where are you driving me? I told you to take me to Hammersmith." The cabman, speechless with astonishment, turned round and made for Hammersmith once more, only however to discover on arriving there, that his "fare" had disappeared again. He became convinced that his cab was haunted, and this belief was strengthened, as he drove back through Kensington by discovering suddenly that his fare was sitting calmly in his vehicle as if nothing had happened. Cabby did not utter a word, for he was too frightened to address his "fare," but drove to the club, where he had picked him up, as quickly as possible. There the young peer alighted, and, without the slightest explanation, paid the cabman five times his fare.

## CHAPTER III

Hansom invents a cab—Chapman designs and patents the present hansom—Francis Moore's vehicles—The Hansom patent infringed —Litigation a failure—Pirate cabs called "shofuls"—The "Clarence" or four-wheeler introduced—An unpleasant fare—The decoration of cabs—Cabmen compelled to wear badges—The "Tribus"—The "Curricle Tribus"—The "Quartobus."

THE prevalence of "bilking" made the back-door cab such an unprofitable vehicle that a new style of cab became imperative.

At the close of 1834, Mr. Joseph Aloysius Hansom, the architect of the old Birmingham Town Hall and founder of *The Builder*, patented a cab designed by himself. The body of this vehicle was almost square and hung in the centre of a square frame. The frame enclosed the whole of the body, passing over and under it. The driver sat on a small seat on the top at the front. The doors were also at the front, one on each side of the cabby's feet. The wheels were seven feet six inches in height—a trifle taller than the vehicle itself—and were attached to the sides of the frame by a pair of short axles. This extraordinary vehicle Mr. Hansom himself drove from Hinckley in Leicestershire to London, much to the wonder of the inhabitants of the various

THE FIRST HANSOM.

towns and villages through which he passed, and to the amusement of the stage-coach drivers and waggoners whom he met on the road. Mr. Hansom, who was financed by Mr. William Boulnois, the inventor of the back-door cab, also registered another cab, the body of which resembled the one just mentioned in every respect, except that the doors were at the sides, and passengers had to enter the vehicle *through* the wheels, which were without felloes, naves, and spokes, the rotary action being produced by a somewhat complicated arrangement of zones and friction rollers. This cab never plied for hire in the streets, but the first-mentioned one, after the wheels had been reduced considerably in size, and one or two minor alterations made, was thought so highly of that a company was formed to purchase Mr. Hansom's rights for £10,000. An old print of this cab represents the passenger exclaiming :—

> "The sweet little cherub that sits up aloft
> Takes care of the fate of poor Jack."

Not a penny of the £10,000 was, however, paid to Hansom, for it was found, as soon as the cabs were placed on the streets, that they were far from being perfect.

The only money Hansom received, directly or indirectly, from his invention was £300, presented to him some time later for services rendered to the company at a critical period. But although he reaped very little pecuniary benefit from his invention, posterity has been generous in connecting his name with a cab which is far superior to the one which he invented. If the cab known to us as the "Hansom" were called the "Chapman," it would be more in accordance with historical accuracy. Mr. John Chapman, the projector of

AN IMPROVED HANSOM.

the Great Indian Peninsular Railway, was, when Mr. Hansom patented his cab, the secretary of the Safety Cabriolet and Two-wheel Carriage Company. He discovered quickly the weak points in Hansom's cab, and, setting to work, invented a far superior one. The driver's seat was placed at the back, the sliding window still in use was introduced, and the framework under the body of the vehicle was constructed to rest on the ground when tilted forwards or backwards. A cranked axle passing under the body of the cab was also introduced.

This cab was patented by Mr. Chapman and Mr. Gillett, who financed him, in December, 1836.

The company which owned Hansom's cab purchased Messrs. Chapman and Gillett's patent, and in a very short time placed fifty of the new cabs on the streets. From the first they were a great success, and for sixty-six years they have remained in public favour. The only important alteration made during those years was the introduction of the straight axle, which necessitated the cutting away of the body of the cab beneath the passenger's seat. This improvement was made very soon after the first Chapman or Hansom appeared on the streets. The side windows of hansoms were, until the fifties, very small—about one foot by eight inches.

Hansom's cab, before being improved by Chapman, bore a strong resemblance to a vehicle of which there is an illustration in Pennant's "London," published in 1790. This vehicle is represented as having just passed under Temple Bar, on which are fixed the gruesome heads of traitors. Knight mentions, in his work on London, having seen a print, dated early in the nineteenth century, of a very similar conveyance, which was

FRANCIS MOORE'S VEHICLE.

described as "the carriage of the ingenious Mr. Moore." That the vehicle in Pennant was built by Francis Moore, of Cheapside, a well-known coachbuilder, there can be no doubt. The difficulty is to decide which conveyance the Pennant picture represents. The *Gentleman's Magazine* for 1771 contains the following paragraph:— "Oct. 30. One of Mr. Moore's carts to carry the mail, upon a new construction, was drawn to the General Post Office. The wheels are eight feet eight inches high, and the body is hung in the same manner as his coal carts, covered with wood, and painted green; the driver is to sit on the top."

Moore patented a two-wheel carriage in June, 1786, and another in 1790. The specifications of the latter show that it was hung on two large wheels. The door, however, was at the back, and the driver had a separate seat at the front, but not on the top of the vehicle. It is very probable that Hansom saw Francis Moore's carriages, and that the cab, which has made his name a household word, was an improvement upon the conveyance depicted in Pennant.

Hansom's original cabs, when not plying for hire, stood on premises which now form a part of the Baker Street Bazaar.

In 1836, hackney-coaches, "outrigger" cabriolets, and back-door cabs were still plying for hire, but the immediate and continued success of Chapman's cab prompted the proprietors of those decaying vehicles to start similar conveyances. Cabs painted and lettered in close imitation of the new patented vehicle were soon as plentiful as the real ones. Some proprietors, who prided themselves on being very smart, always had the word "not" painted in very small letters before the inscription, "Hansom's Patent Safety," believing that this would save them from being prosecuted. They were mistaken, for the company made a determined effort to protect its rights, and commenced legal proceedings against the infringers of its patent. In every case the company was successful, and heavy damages were awarded it, but the victories were barren ones, for on almost every occasion the infringer of the patent turned out to be a man of straw. So when the Company had spent £2000 in lawsuits, and had succeeded only in obtaining payment of one fine of £500, it came to the conclusion that the wisest thing it could do would be to refrain in future from litigation. That was a splendid thing for the "pirate" cabs, who now dispensed with the word "not," and appeared similar in every respect to the real "Hansoms," as the Chapmans were called. When the company took over Chapman's cabs it had painted on them

"Hansom's Patent Safety," so that the public might know that the conveyances belonged to the same firm as the cab which Hansom invented. And the result of this absurd action on the part of the company is that Hansom enjoys the fame which belongs by right to Chapman.

Although few people could distinguish a real hansom from its many imitators, the Company's drivers knew the difference, and treated "pirate" cabs with the utmost contempt. They called them "shofuls," and many ingenious explanations of the origin of that word have been published during the last fifty years. Some people declared that a hansom closely resembled a shovel, while others explained that two persons in a cab made it a "show full." As a matter of fact, "shoful" was a slang word for "counterfeit" among the lower class Jews, and was conferred by the many Jewish employés of the Company upon those vehicles which infringed Hansom's or Chapman's patent. In course of time it became the slang term for all hansoms, but the word is now very rarely heard.

The first four-wheeler was placed upon the streets, just as Chapman's cab appeared, by the

General Cabriolet Conveyance Company. It was built by Mr. David Davies, the builder of the cabriolets of 1823, was called a "covered cab," and carried two passengers inside and one on the box seat. The doors were at the sides. This cab was quickly improved upon, and the "Clarence," our much-abused "growler," was the result. Lord Brougham was highly pleased with

THE FIRST FOUR-WHEELED CAB.

the new vehicle, and in 1840 he instructed his coachbuilder—Mr. Robinson of Mount Street—to make him one of a superior description. Hence the brougham.

Elderly and sober-minded people showed a marked preference for riding in clarences, and hansoms soon became considered the vehicles of the fast and disreputable. This reputation has not been lived down entirely, for, at the present day, there are some old ladies who will on no account enter a hansom, and shake their heads sorrowfully when they see their grand-daughters doing so. It must be confessed that hansoms figured in police-court cases much more frequently than the four-wheelers did. A well-known cab proprietor, who died a few years ago, had, in his youth, an exceedingly unpleasant experience while driving a hansom. One night he was hailed by two men who were supporting between them a sailor, who was, apparently, in an advanced state of intoxication. They placed the sailor in the cab, and then, turning to the cabman, told him to drive to a certain quiet place some distance away and wait for them there. They explained that they had a brief call to make and could not take the drunken man with them, but they would follow on in less than a quarter of an hour, and inspired confidence by paying a portion of the fare in advance. Cabby drove off and all went well until reaching a toll-gate. As the keeper came out of the toll-house he caught sight of the sailor, and, thinking that something was the matter with him, he went closer and peered into his face. Then he ran to the horse's head, and seizing it, exclaimed sharply to the cabman, "Hallo! young fellow, you've got a stiff 'un in there."

"Go on; he's only drunk," the cabman replied. But the toll-keeper was not satisfied with the explanation, and detained the cab until a policeman arrived. The sailor was then examined, and it was at once evident that not only was he dead, but that he had been so for several days. It was, in fact, a body-snatching job, and the rascals engaged in it had dressed the corpse in sailor's clothes to get it through the streets without attracting attention. Instructed by the police, the cabman drove to the place where he had been told to await the men, but they did not appear to claim the body. They had evidently kept a distant watch on the cab.

In the thirties and forties cabs were painted in most startling and conflicting colours, the proprietors considering, apparently, that the greater the contrast the more effective the result. A miniature white horse, symbolic of the House of Hanover, was painted on the majority of hansoms. On the sides of four-wheelers were depicted strange monsters unknown to heraldry, zoology, or mythology. These were in imitation of the armorial bearings so conspicuous on the panels of the old hackney-coaches, which, as already stated, were generally discarded family coaches.

In 1838, cabmen were compelled by Act of Parliament to take out a licence and wear a badge. On the day of the distribution of badges, many of the cabmen, attired in their best clothes, took a holiday. Some half a dozen of them walked along the Strand with their badges fixed conspicuously on their chests. A crowd soon collected around them, and in it were two Frenchmen, one apparently showing the other the sights of London. The latter inquired who the cabmen were, and an Englishman, who understood French, was surprised to hear the following reply :—

"They are gentlemen who have been decorated by the Government in honour of Her Majesty's coronation."

A new hansom, the "Tribus," patented by Mr. Harvey of Lambeth House, Westminster-bridge Road, was placed on the streets in 1844, but it was not well patronised and was soon withdrawn. The "Tribus" carried three passengers, and the entrance was at the rear, the driver's seat being removed further to the "off-side." The cabman was thus able to open or shut the door without descending from his seat. There were five windows to the vehicle, two being in front, one on each side, and one behind—beneath the driver's seat. Small safety wheels—such as can be seen at the present day attached to many

THE TRIBUS. BACK VIEW.

omnibuses—were fixed to the front of the "Tribus" to prevent the vehicle pitching forward in the event of the horse falling, a shaft breaking, or a wheel coming off.

Mr. Harvey also patented the "Curricle Tribus," a vehicle similar to the "Tribus," with the exception that it was drawn by two horses abreast, did not possess safety wheels, and could be converted at pleasure into an open carriage. The "Curricle Tribus," however, never plied for hire.

Another unsuccessful cab was the "Quartobus,"

THE TRIBUS. SIDE VIEW.

a four-wheeler with accommodation for four inside passengers. It was introduced in 1844, and Mr. Okey, the inventor, described it as "hung on four wheels, the coupling being very close for easy draft."

## CHAPTER IV

A strike—Cabmen's revenge on Members of Parliament—Cab radius altered—Cabmen object to knocking at doors—The King of Cabmen—Nicknames—A lady feared by cabmen—The kilometric reckoner—Lord John Russell and "Palace Yard Jack"—Cab fares altered—A strike against the introduction of lamps—Another strike—The Cab-drivers' Benevolent Association—The London Cabmen's Mission—The Hackney Carriage Proprietors' Provident Institution—The Cabmen's Shelter Fund.

THE cabmen's reputation for being extortionate is by no means of recent growth, but frequently men have been accused wrongfully. In 1853, a cabman was charged with demanding more than his legal fare, the complainant declaring that although the distance travelled was only three miles the defendant had charged as if it were five. Cabby was sentenced to a month's imprisonment, but before his time expired a gentleman interested himself in his case, and paid to have the distance officially measured. It was seven miles!

In the same year the Government imposed fresh regulations upon cabs, and the fares, which had been eightpence a mile, and fourpence for every additional half a mile, or portion of half a mile, were reduced to sixpence for every mile, and for any part of a mile over and above any number of miles completed. Mr. Thompson of Southampton Row, a proprietor in a large way of business, had introduced those fares two years previously.

The new regulations and the reduction of fares created great indignation among both cab proprietors and cab drivers. The latter were particularly enraged with the Members of Parliament, and hit upon a way of expressing publicly their feelings towards them. When the House rose on the night of July 26, and the members hurried out to go home, they were astonished to see all the cabmen drive quickly away with empty cabs. Some of them ran after the cabs; but the drivers declined in most unparliamentary language to take them, and as many of the honourable gentlemen who could not get a lift in friends' carriages had to walk home. The following morning there was not a cab to be seen in the streets of London, for the cabmen were on strike. Members of Parliament soon felt the want of cabs, and the Sergeant-at-Arms personally asked Mr. Gamble, an omnibus proprietor, to oblige them by running an omnibus for their sole convenience between the House and the clubs. But Mr. Gamble, who was also a cab proprietor, and not just then very well disposed towards Members of Parliament, declined to accede to their request. The strike, however, only lasted for four days, for when the men saw that the police permitted unlicensed vehicles to ply for hire they returned to work. Nevertheless, they gained something by the strike, for their grievances were investigated without delay, and the following alterations made. The cab radius, which for twenty-four years had been three miles from the General Post Office, was changed to four miles from the statue of Charles I. at Charing Cross, and the cabman was empowered to charge one shilling for every mile, or part of one, which he should be required to drive beyond the radius, providing that the cab was discharged beyond it. Moreover, the tax on each cab was reduced from ten shillings a week to a shilling a day.

The success which attended the first cab strike of any importance incited cabmen to think of other grievances, and from that year to this they have never been without a good supply of them. Some were reasonable, but the majority were imaginary or frivolous. Of the latter nothing need be said. Of the former, one of the chief was that passengers expected cabmen to get down and ring the bell or knock at the door of the house where they wished to alight. For years the cabmen's objection to performing this duty was a source of continual squabbles, and consequent police-court cases. But at length one magistrate decided that cabmen were not obliged to ring bells or knock at doors. Other magistrates agreed with him and cabmen were jubilant. But an old gentleman, who used cabs daily, objected strongly to the new arrangement and determined to teach the cabmen a lesson. One cold winter's evening, he hired a cab and rode home—a shilling distance. On arriving at his destination, he requested the cabman to knock at the street door. But cabby declined to do so. "This is a free country," he said, "and knocking at doors ain't no part of my duty."

"Very well, then," the old gentleman replied, looking at his watch, "by the law of this free country I sentence you to remain idle, in the cold, for fourteen minutes, without any addition to your fare." Then he went indoors and did not send out his shilling until fourteen minutes had elapsed, for he knew that no waiting fare could be charged until fifteen minutes had passed. Afterwards he informed the London newspapers of what he had done, and suggested that their readers should follow his example. Hundreds did, and the squabbles between cabmen and their "fares" became more frequent than ever. For some years the quarrel dragged on, but finally people ceased from commanding cabmen to knock at doors, and when they particularly wished it done they asked for it as a favour.

Another grievance of cabmen, before shelters were built for their convenience, was the action of the police in summoning them for leaving their cabs outside coffee-shops while having their dinner. "The King of Cabmen," a well-dressed, important-looking individual, whom the public believed to be an aristocrat, although he was really the son of a London tailor, protested publicly against their action by dining *al fresco* in the leading thoroughfares. He would pull up outside some public-house or dining place in the Strand, Oxford Street,

Haymarket, Regent Street, or Piccadilly, spread a very clean table-cloth over the top of his cab, and have his dinner brought out to him. Frequently he dined outside West-end clubs, his dinner being sent out by members who sympathised with him. "The King of Cabmen" was also known as "Nonpareil." When sixpenny fares were introduced, "Nonpareil" took a prominent part in denouncing the action of the Government, and whenever a passenger offered him sixpence he haughtily suggested tossing him "double or quits."

Cabmen have always been fond of bestowing nicknames upon their comrades, and at the present day there are men named "Busy Bee," "Dan, the policeman," "Engineer Charley," "Piggy," "Nicodemus," "Bill King about Jermyn Street," "Harry of Halfmoon Street," "Father Christmas," "Hospital Jack," "Rhoderic Dhu," "Old Pickles," "Topsy," "Bustler," "Old London," "Australian Jack," "Candle-dipper," "Mr. Smith," "Doctor," "Sloane Square Sailor Jack," and "Joe in the Copper." Cabmen also bestow nicknames upon their masters, the cab proprietors, and, in the majority of cases, they are of an uncomplimentary nature. Those existing at the present day must remain unknown beyond the circle of cabmen, but there is no harm in publishing nicknames applied to proprietors long since dead. "Whooping-cough Bill" was so named because he filled up pauses in his conversation with nervous little coughs. "Pious Tommy" would allow no swearing in his yards. "Jack the giant-killer" was barely five feet two in height. "Darling Joey" had been married three times. "Skin 'em alive" never allowed his men any credit, and "Boozey Bill" was a teetotaler. Cab proprietresses usually were named from something striking about their personal appearance. "Ginger Sal" needs no explanation. "Beautiful Kate" was exceedingly plain, and "Fairy Emma" was so stout that she could scarcely walk. Another woman, very good-looking, but domineering and detested by all cabmen who had business transactions with her, was known throughout London as "The Queen of Hell."

There was another woman, not an owner of cabs, who was feared by all the cabmen of London, and consequently had more uncomplimentary names bestowed upon her than any other woman ever had. Mrs. Prodgers, the lady in question, obtained considerable fame through her constant squabbles with cabmen. Possessing an extensive and unique knowledge of cab law and London mileage, she made a point of travelling the full distance to which her shilling entitled her, with the result that cabmen who did not know her usually demanded more than the legal fare. Her reply was to take his number, and apply for a summons against him. Frequently she summoned men who took what she offered without demur, for she had practically appointed herself an inspector of cabs and cabmen, and was as successful in discovering breaches of the hackney-carriage regulations as the most energetic paid official could have been. After a time she became so dreaded that the warning cry of "Mother Prodgers" would send every cab within hail dashing away up side streets to escape her. Even now there are scores of cabmen who cannot hear her name mentioned without fuming with indignation.

The conditions of a cabman's employment were, and still are, calculated to encourage extortion. The cabby paid the owner a certain amount for the loan of his cab, and his profits did not begin until he had earned the hire money. Therefore, when a cabman, after waiting for hours on the rank, obtained a "fare," the temptation to overcharge was very great. It was his first job that day, and it might be his last. He was grateful for an extra shilling or sixpence, but if it were not offered to him he endeavoured to obtain it by indulging in scathing remarks or vulgar abuse. The fact that a cabman has a wife and children to support may be considered extenuating circumstances, but it is poor consolation for the unfortunate victims of his extortion.

With the idea of protecting the public against overcharge, an endeavour was made, in 1858, to get attached to cabs a patent machine named "The Kilometric Register," which would indicate the number of miles travelled and the fare to be paid. But the cabmen objected strongly to such an innovation, and it was not made.

Lord John Russell was in the habit of riding home every night from the House of Commons in a cab. The distance was short, and the cabmen all knew that he paid a shilling for his ride. But one night a cabman, well known as "Palace Yard Jack," was surprised to find that Lord John had placed a sovereign in his hand instead of a shilling. He saw that the statesman had made a mistake, but having had a spell of bad luck, and being in great need of a new pair of boots, he did not call his lordship's attention to the coin. But on the following night, as "Palace Yard Jack" was sitting on his cab, Lord John Russell walked up to him, and said :—

"You drove me home last night, I think."

"Yes, my lord."

"What did I give you?"

"A sovereign, my lord."

"Well, what have you done with it?"

"Bought a new pair of boots; and"—sticking out his feet—"look, my lord, they're Russells, not Wellingtons."

Lord John Russell smiled and walked away, leaving "Palace Yard Jack" to boast of his smartness.

In 1860 there were upwards of 4300 licensed cabs in London, and 200 cabstands.

Three years later Mr. Thomas Tilling started four cabs, and at the present day his successors, Thomas Tilling, Limited, possess over sixty.

The minimum cab fare of one shilling was

introduced in 1867. For that sum a passenger could ride two miles, the fare for any additional distance ridden being sixpence a mile or part of a mile. This abolition of sixpenny fares gave great satisfaction to cabmen; but another regulation filled them with indignation. In December, 1867, Parliament gave power to the Chief Commissioner of Police to insist upon all cabs carrying, between sunset and sunrise, "at least one lamp properly trimmed and lighted." Hansoms, or the majority of them, had for many years carried a lamp, but the proprietors and drivers of four-wheelers protested strongly against being put to the expense while vans and private carriages were permitted to be without lights. The hansom drivers supported the four-wheeler men, and on December 3 the whole of the cabmen went on strike. A promise was immediately made that the Police order should not be enforced, and on December 5 the men returned to work. However, two years later Parliament passed an Act compelling all cabs to carry a lighted lamp from sunset to sunrise.

The next strike began in September, 1868, and was an attempt to compel the Railway

Companies to abolish the "privilege" system and admit all cabs to their termini. It was, however, shortlived and unsuccessful.

On January 1, 1870, a new regulation, compelling all cab proprietors to display inside their vehicles a list of fares, came into force. Four-wheelers were to have them fixed or painted on their doors; hansoms, facing the passengers. By the same Act the cost of licences was reduced from £19 and £17 to £2 2*s*.

In the same year the Cab-drivers' Benevolent Association was founded, to make some provision for deserving aged or infirm cabmen unable to earn their living. The late Marquis of Townshend, a staunch friend of cabmen, took an active part in establishing it, and for many years it was known among cabbies as "The Marquis's Society." The objects of the Association, of which His Majesty the King is patron, are (1) to give annuities of £20 each to aged cab-drivers who from infirmity are unable to earn their living; (2) to grant loans, without interest, to members requiring such aid, and to give temporary assistance to those who may be in distress through unavoidable causes; (3) to give legal assistance to members who may be unjustly summoned to the police-courts.

In 1900 the Society had sixty-five annuitants, and also granted small loans to seventy-six members, nearly the whole of which were repaid.

Cabmen becoming members while under thirty years of age pay an annual subscription of 5*s.* and an entrance fee of 2*s.* If over thirty the entrance fee is 3*s.* There is also a Widow and Orphan Relief Fund, for which an additional subscription of 2*s.* a-year has to be paid.

At the annual meeting of the Society in March, 1900, Benjamin Heppelthwaite, aged 74, was elected one of the annuitants; but, feeling that he was still able to work, he waived his right to the annuity, which was then given to the highest unsuccessful candidate. Heppelthwaite's generous behaviour did not go unrewarded. The chairman, Viscount Duncannon, at once announced that he would give Heppelthwaite, for the next twelve months, a sum equal to the annuity which he had refused in favour of a weaker friend.

In 1871 the London Cabmen's Mission was started in premises adjoining the King's Cross Station of the Metropolitan Railway, and during the thirty years of its existence has done much to improve the moral character of cabmen. Religious services for cabmen and their families are held at the hall at King's Cross on four days in each week, and the missionary also visits the men on the ranks to talk with them and distribute bright, wholesome magazines.

We read, frequently, in the daily papers, of cabmen being drunk while at work, and it will, therefore, surprise many people to hear that there is a large number of total abstainers among London cab-drivers. During the summer months a cabmen's Gospel Temperance meeting is held every Sunday evening on the stand outside King's Cross Railway Station. The speakers and singers are all cabmen. Last year they held, at the same spot, an open-air Harvest Festival. Fruit, flowers, vegetables and bread were displayed on the temporary platform, and a cabman sang, "Oh, what shall the harvest be?" At the conclusion of the service the fruit, flowers, and other gifts, were taken in cabs and given to a Rescue Home.

The London Cabmen's Mission also distributes among the men, woollen mufflers, cuffs and hosiery —presents which are greatly appreciated. One lady subscriber gave the Mission six dozen sun-bonnets for cab-horses, and thereby added to the comfort of the animals and the gaiety of the streets.

Another very excellent society, the "Hackney Carriage Proprietors' Provident Fund," was founded, by the late Mr. Herbert Rymill, in April, 1873. It was started to establish a fund for providing annuities of £26 to aged, decayed, or disabled cab proprietors or their widows, and to afford temporary relief to its members or to the widows and children of deceased members. It was registered under the Friendly Societies Acts in July, 1878, and in January, 1887, its title was changed to the "Hackney Carriage Proprietors' Provident Institution." For an annual subscription of £1 1*s.* a member is able to make provision against misfortune. Many a cab proprietor has, through no fault of his own, been reduced from comfortable circumstances to want. One of his horses may have contracted glanders in consequence of the driver foolishly permitting it to drink at a public trough; the disease spreads through his stables and a number of his horses have to be destroyed. To a wealthy cab proprietor this is a serious loss, but to a man who owns only three or four cabs it would mean ruin but for the "Hackney Carriage Proprietors' Provident Institution's" assistance in helping him to tide over his difficulties. And it must be remembered that the majority of cab proprietors are small owners; on December 31, 1900, there were 2782 licensed cab proprietors in London, and of these 2207 owned from one to five vehicles.

The "Hackney Carriage Proprietors' Provident Institution" had been in existence barely two years when the "Cabmen's Shelter Fund" was started. Its object was to provide for cabmen on the ranks a place where they could obtain protection from the weather, and purchase good, wholesome food at moderate prices.

On February 6, 1875, the first shelter for London cabmen was opened in Acacia Road, St. John's Wood, by the Hon. Arthur Kinnaird, M.P., Vice-President of the Society. Among the crowd which had assembled to witness the ceremony were some thirty or forty cabmen who came, as representatives of their class, to do honour to the occasion. By the end of the year the Society had placed thirteen shelters in various parts of the

Metropolis, and, at the present time, it possesses forty-three, a dozen of which are open day and night. Many of these were presented to the Society; the one in Palace Yard, Westminster, by members of both Houses of Parliament, and those at Pont Street, Belgrave Square, St. George's Square, S.W., Clapham Common, Kensington Crescent, Royal Crescent, Uxbridge Road, Piccadilly, Warwick Road, Maida Vale, and the one near the Oratory, Brompton Road, by residents in those neighbourhoods. The shelter at Portland Road Station was presented by the residents of Richmond. The remainder were either erected by the Fund or presented to it by various individuals. The entire cost of the new shelter now being erected in the Haymarket has been defrayed by Sir Squire Bancroft.

The forty-three shelters maintained by the Society are used daily by nearly four thousand cabmen. The attendants in charge of the various shelters make their living by selling provisions to the frequenters, and cooking, at a charge of one penny, any food they may bring in.

Every shelter is divided into two compartments—a mess-room and a small kitchen. The mess-rooms are supplied with newspapers, and some of them possess small libraries.

In the mess-rooms the following rules are displayed :—

1. This Shelter is the property of the Cabmen's Shelter Fund and is for the use of CAB-DRIVERS solely.
2. The Drivers of the FIRST TWO CABS on the rank are not to enter the Shelter.
3. No bad language, card-playing, betting, or gambling allowed.
4. The Attendant in charge is authorised to sell Tea, Coffee, and Bread and Butter to the Drivers using the Shelter only, at prices as per Tariff.
5. The Attendant is instructed to see that the above Rules are strictly kept.

Any complaints as to attendance, quality of refreshments sold, etc., etc., must be made to the Hon. Sec., and will be at once attended to.

The Committee appeal to the good sense and feeling of the Drivers to help in maintaining the respectability of this Shelter, and by every means in their power to prevent its being damaged.

During one of the recent cab strikes an attempt was made at some shelters to prevent non-strikers from using them. This was, of course, in direct opposition to the rules of the Society, and the strikers were taught that the shelters are for all cab-drivers.

## CHAPTER V

Cab show at Alexandra Palace—Forder's cab—The strike of 1894—Cabmen become organ-grinders—The Asquith award—Boycotting the railway stations—The "Bilking Act."

On October 4, 1875, a Cab and Cab-Horse Show was opened at the Alexandra Palace, and attracted a large number of people to Muswell Hill. The first prize for the most convenient and best appointed hansom cab was awarded to Messrs. Forder, who also exhibited one of the same type which they had built for the Prince of Wales. Two years previously, a cab built by this firm had been awarded the Gold Medal of the Society of Arts, and this identical hansom won at the Alexandra Palace the second prize for vehicles which had been at work for not less than six months. Forder's cab had been working in the London streets for two years.

In the class for horses which had been at cab work for not less than eight years, during which they must have been the property of the exhibitor, the first prize was won by Mrs. Ruth Farmer, whose bay mare, aged twenty, had been in constant work for seventeen years.

Prizes were also offered for cabmen who had retained their badges and been exempt for the longest period from any charge of cruelty to animals, reckless driving, drunkenness or any other offence, and who had constantly driven for upwards of ten years. The winner of the first prize had been a cab-driver for forty-six years.

The long service and good conduct prize was awarded to a cabman who had been for thirty-five years in the service of his master, and the Temperance prize was won by a driver who had been a teetotaler for twenty-nine years.

Strikes, and threats to strike, have been exceedingly numerous since 1853. On some occasions the cabmen objected to Government regulations, and on others their quarrels were with the cab proprietors. It had been the complaint of cabmen, for very many years, that the prices charged by proprietors for the hire of their cabs were too high, and in May, 1894, they determined to make a strenuous effort to get them reduced.

On the morning of May 10 they held a meeting in a hall at Bell Street, Edgware Road, to discuss the advisability of striking, in the event of the cab owners refusing to accede to their demands, the chief of which was that the hiring-price of 16*s*. or 17*s*. a day should be reduced by three shillings. The meeting was enthusiastic, and decided, promptly, to strike unless the cab proprietors made the reduction which they wanted. Negotiations were then opened with the cab proprietors, who refused, however, to comply with the men's request, pointing out, in support of their decision, that, as a large number of cabmen never worked more than four or five days a week, it was evident that they made a very good living, and could, if they liked, make a still better one.

In consequence of the cab proprietors' attitude, a mass meeting was held at midnight on May 14 at the Novelty Theatre, and the place was so crowded that an overflow meeting had to be held in the street. The resolution, pledging the men to strike, was moved and carried with tremendous enthusiasm by both meetings. The following morning the strike began, but, contrary to the expectation of most people, there were many cabs plying for hire. The majority of these belonged to proprietors in a small way of business who had submitted to the Union's demands and were permitted, therefore, to run. Men who drove their own cabs were also allowed to work, but both class of vehicles had to affix the Union's labels on their windows. The former bore the legend, "Fair-priced cab," while the latter carried an announcement that they were working by permission of the Union. Three thousand Union labels were issued, and, as far as the public was concerned, the strike was not very serious. There was a little difficulty at the railway stations on the first day about getting sufficient cabs, and some people complained that they could not procure them after the theatres closed. Considering, however, that nearly nine thousand cabs were kept off the streets, it is truly surprising that far greater inconvenience was not caused to the public. Many people said it was a conclusive sign that at ordinary times there are far too many cabs in London. Of course, the cabs which were permitted by the Union to run earned plenty of money, but the drivers were not allowed to keep all of it. Those who worked were expected to contribute towards the support of those who did not, and, for once in a way, that was a perfectly fair arrangement. Certain of the men on strike were sent out daily by the Union to sell tickets to the men at work. These tickets were of various prices, and the colour indicated their value. When a cabman bought one he stuck it in his hat, so that his fellowmen might see to what extent he was doing his duty. But selling tickets was by no means the only way in which the Union raised money to carry on the strike. Cabmen were sent out with street organs, and for many days ground out music from morning till night with very satisfactory results—from a pecuniary point of view. 'Busmen chaffed them unmercifully about these organs for many months after, and an argument between a cabby and a 'busman invariably ended in the latter advising the former to take his cab home and bring out his organ.

When the strike had lasted for nearly a month, a Board of Conciliation was formed to settle, if possible, the dispute. Cab proprietors and strikers were both represented, the Home Secretary (Mr. H. H. Asquith) acting as mediator. After a few meetings had been held at the House of Commons,

Mr. Asquith made his award, which was as follows :—

| | | | | | | |
|---|---|---|---|---|---|---|
| June 4 to | July 15, | 6 weeks | at | 16*s*. | per | day. |
| July 16 ,, | ,, 22, | 1 ,, | ,, | 15*s*. | ,, | ,, |
| ,, 23 ,, | ,, 29, | 1 ,, | ,, | 14*s*. | ,, | ,, |
| ,, 30 ,, | August 5, | 1 ,, | ,, | 13*s*. | ,, | ,, |
| August 6 ,, | ,, 12, | 1 ,, | ,, | 12*s*. | ,, | ,, |
| ,, 13 ,, | ,, 19, | 1 ,, | ,, | 11*s*. | ,, | ,, |
| ,, 20 ,, | October 21, | 9 ,, | ,, | 10*s*. | ,, | ,, |
| October 22 ,, | ,, 28, | 1 ,, | ,, | 11*s*. | ,, | ,, |
| ,, 29 ,, | January 14, | 11 ,, | ,, | 12*s*. | ,, | ,, |
| January 15 ,, | April 1, | 11 ,, | ,, | 11*s*. | ,, | ,, |
| April 2 ,, | ,, 15, | 2 ,, | ,, | 12*s*. | ,, | ,, |
| ,, 16 ,, | May 6, | 3 ,, | ,, | 13*s*. | ,, | ,, |
| May 7 ,, | ,, 20, | 2 ,, | ,, | 14*s*. | ,, | ,, |
| ,, 21 ,, | June 3, | 2 ,, | ,, | 15*s*. | ,, | ,, |

"The above scale is to regulate the net cash price to be paid per day by driver to owner for first-class street hansom cabs from this date. It is to be subject to revision as from the first Monday in April, 1895, if within fourteen days prior to that date notice demanding revision is given to me by, or on behalf of, either of the parties to the agreement of this day."

The award was dated June 11, 1894, and two days later the cabmen went back to work. On the 27th of the same month Mr. Asquith fixed the following scale for four-wheeled cabs :—

(1) The net cash price to be paid by driver to owner for best street iron-tyred four-wheeled cabs, with two horses per day, to be according to the subjoined scale :—

| | | | | |
|---|---|---|---|---|
| May 14 to | July 22, | 10 weeks | at 13*s*. | per day. |
| July 23 ,, | August 12, | 3 ,, | ,, 12*s*. | ,, ,, |
| August 13 ,, | September 9, | 4 ,, | ,, 11*s*. | ,, ,, |
| September 10 ,, | March 26, | 28 ,, | ,, 10*s*. | ,, ,, |
| March 27 ,, | April 9, | 2 ,, | ,, 11*s*. | ,, ,, |
| April 10 ,, | May 14, | 5 ,, | ,, 12*s*. | ,, ,, |

(2) The net cash price to be paid by driver to owner for rubber-tyred four-wheeled cabs to be in all cases 1*s*. (one shilling) over the price for iron-tyred four-wheeled cabs.

(3) The net cash price to be paid by driver to owner for four-wheeled cabs worked on the one-horse principle to be according to the subjoined scale :—

| | | | | |
|---|---|---|---|---|
| June 4 to | July 29, | 8 weeks | at 8*s*. | per day |
| July 30 ,, | April 2, | 35 ,, | ,, 6*s*. 6*d*. | ,, ,, |
| April 3 ,, | May 7, | 5 ,, | ,, 7*s*. | ,, ,, |
| May 8 ,, | June 3, | 4 ,, | ,, 7*s*. 6*d*. | ,, ,, |

(4) The actual amount charged by the Railway Companies for privileged cabs to be paid by the drivers to the owners in addition to the above.

Londoners were heartily glad when the strike was at an end ; not because they had suffered very much inconvenience from it, but out of sympathy for the women and children, for strike pay is not magnificent. Nevertheless, over a thousand men were thankful to receive it for many weeks after the strike was concluded. These were men who found themselves out of work through cab proprietors having sold off their stock and retired from business in disgust. The balance-sheet of the Cab-drivers' Union dealing with the strike showed that £8202 was received, and £8111 spent from the beginning of the strike until July 28.

The next strike began in September, 1896, and aimed at compelling the Railway Companies to allow all cabs the privilege of entering their termini to pick up fares. The drivers refused to work for any proprietor who had privileged cabs, and pressure was put upon the drivers of the latter vehicles to cease work until the Railways agreed to the Union's demands. The number that did so, however, was comparatively small. Then the strikers made the great mistake of trying to get the public on their side by inconveniencing it. They refused to take people into any terminus in which they were not allowed to pick up fares, but put them down, luggage and all, outside the premises. But, to their surprise, they found that their fares refused to pay unless they were taken right into the station. So that plan was discarded very quickly. The strike dragged on for many weeks, but the average Londoner only knew that it existed by seeing Union mottoes adorning the cabmen's whips. Eventually it died peacefully of sheer weakness.

The year of this futile strike saw the passing of an Act which was badly needed. Although "bilking" has never been so common as it was in the days of back-door cabs, there has always been a number of well-dressed rascals who make a point of swindling cabmen. Usually they alight at some big shop or institution, telling the cab-driver that they will be out again in a few minutes and will want to be taken farther; then they enter the building and pass out by another door into a different street, leaving the cabman to discover that he has been "bilked." The "Bilking Act," as cabmen call the Act of 1896, made any person who hired a cab knowing that he could not pay the legal fare, or intending to avoid payment of it, liable to a fine of 40*s*., in addition to the fare, or to be imprisoned for a term not exceeding fourteen days. The whole or part of the fine could be given to the cabman as compensation.

## CHAPTER VI

Gentlemen cabmen—An applicant's nerve—The doctor-cabby—John Cockram—A drunken cabman's horse.

CAB proprietors receive applications for work from all classes of men. One morning a particularly dissipated-looking fellow strolled into a cab-yard, not far from King's Cross, and asked the proprietor for a job, mentioning that he had driven most things in India from a pony-trap to a four-in-hand, and did not anticipate the slightest difficulty in driving a cab. The proprietor observed that it required some nerve to drive a cab in London. "Nerve!" the applicant exclaimed. "Well, I don't think I'm deficient in that. One morning in India I woke and found a cobra coiled up on my bed. It wasn't a nice position to find myself in, but I'd been in many a worse fix and didn't lose my presence of mind. I'm a bit of ventriloquist, and as there was a big image of some old Hindoo god at the other end of the room I immediately made it speak. As I expected, directly the cobra heard the voice he slipped off the bed like a shot and went for the idol, while I seized the opportunity to bolt from the room." The cab proprietor congratulated him on his presence of mind, but after appearing to consult a well-worn book, declared that he had not a single vacancy. The applicant did not seem very disappointed, and having succeeded in borrowing twopence, departed.

Many aristocratic, military and professional men have at various times driven a cab for a livelihood, and usually they have been reduced to that strait through their own folly; but there have been cases of young, well-educated men driving cabs for a period until their prospects in life brightened. Only seven or eight years ago a student at one of our great London hospitals passed his "final," and found himself in the painful position of being a qualified medical man without any money. Unable to obtain a *locum tenens* or an assistantship, he applied for and received a cabman's licence. Medical students and their friends made a point of patronising him, and for some months "the doctor" was one of the best-known cabmen in the West End. He has now a very good provincial practice, but the money with which he purchased the nucleus of it was not earned as a cabman. This "doctor" is not the cabman referred to in Chapter IV. The latter, who has been a driver for twenty-one years, is an old man.

An ex-cabman who is well known to many hundreds of Londoners is John Cockram. He was born, in 1833, in French-horn Yard, Holborn, his father being a cab proprietor in a small way of business. Cockram, senior, died early in the forties, leaving a widow and four children totally unprovided for. Moreover, he was deeply in debt to a horse dealer, who speedily caused the stock-in-trade and household furniture to be seized and sold. All that was left to the widow was a bed, a Prayer-book, a Bible, and a watch which had been presented to her by the physician to George IV., in whose service she had been prior to her marriage. Young Cockram, although but eleven years of age, became the main support of his mother, and a few years later she was entirely dependent upon him.

In 1851 John Cockram became a cab-driver,

but as he objected on religious grounds to Sunday work, it was his ambition to possess a cab of his own. Having saved £20, he purchased a horse, hired a cab, and started business on his own account; but, as he followed Mr. Thompson's example and accepted sixpenny fares, he became unpopular with cabmen, and a complaint was

JOHN COCKRAM.

made to Sir Richard Mayne, the Chief Commissioner of Police, that he was driving a cab while under age. But when Sir Richard Mayne discovered that Cockram was the sole support of his mother, and, moreover, thoroughly qualified for a cab-driver in every respect, except age, he declined to prohibit him from driving. However, there was trouble in store for Cockram. He had been a proprietor for a very short time when his horse bolted, and the cab was smashed. Again Cockram had to drive for a master, but this time he refused to drive on Sundays.

"If you don't take the cab out on Sunday, you shan't on Monday," the proprietor declared; but Cockram at once offered to pay him 5*s*. every Saturday night to allow his horse and cab to remain in the yard on the following day. The proprietor agreed to this arrangement, and Cockram drove for him for two years, during which time he paid off the money which he owed for the smashed cab, and began educating himself, while waiting on the rank, by studying *Cassell's Popular Educator*.

In 1860 Cockram competed for and won a prize of £20 offered for the best essay on "Sunday cab-driving, and its influence on the religious, domestic, and physical condition of those employed." Cockram wrote his essay in the streets, using the top of his hansom as a writing-desk. On the essay being published in book form, George Moore, the philanthropist, Sir Hope Grant, and Mr. J. T. Delane, the editor of the *Times*, sent for Cockram, congratulated him on his work, and made many inquiries concerning Sunday cab work. Colonel H. Knollys mentions in his "Life of General Sir Hope Grant," that the General commissioned Cockram to buy him a cheap cab-horse to use in his private hansom, and promised him £5 for his trouble. Cockram purchased a horse for £38, but refused to accept more than £2, his usual charge for such transactions.

Some years later Cockram published a useful little book entitled, "The Horse in Sickness, and how to treat him."

In 1862 Cockram and another young driver started business as cab proprietors. Each had saved £100, and with their joint capital they purchased seven horses, three cabs, and seven sets of harness. The partners were of one opinion concerning Sunday work, and a clause was inserted in their deed of partnership prohibiting either of them from letting out, or using for their own pleasure, on Sunday, any horse or vehicle. They prospered, and in 1877, the year in which they sold their business, they possessed cabs, omnibuses, broughams, traps, and 126 horses.

Since retiring from business Mr. Cockram has been a member of the Richmond Town Council, and the Richmond Board of Guardians, and, in June, 1895, gave evidence before the Select Committee of the House of Lords on the Lord's Day Act.

For many years Cockram has been an active member of the Open Air Mission, and is frequently called upon to speak at meetings of the Working Men's Lord's Day Rest Association, and kindred societies. Although now sixty-eight years of age, he is still very energetic, and when I last saw him—three or four months ago—he was preparing to start off on his bicycle to hold a service many miles away from London.

Drunkenness has been the ruin of many cabmen, and the cause of numerous accidents to the cab-riding public. Some people have had very narrow escapes. Many years ago a lady and gentleman hailed a cab on the Grand Parade, Portsmouth, and told the cabman to drive them to Landport Station. They took no particular notice of the cabman, and on arriving at the station were considerably surprised to see that everybody was staring at them. On proceeding to pay their fare they discovered that the cabman's seat was empty, and the bystanders then informed them that the cab arrived without any driver. The police took up the matter, and discovered eventually that when the cabman picked up his fare he was so intoxicated that before he had driven clear of the High Street he had rolled from his seat into the middle of the road. The horse of its own accord had taken the unsuspecting passengers in safety to their destination.

In London, quite recently, two ladies driving in a hansom had a narrow escape. They were engrossed in conversation when, suddenly, to their surprise, they saw a policeman dash at their horse, and, after a few moments' struggle, bring it to a standstill. A large crowd collected immediately, and not until then did the ladies become aware that their horse had taken fright, that the cabman had been thrown from his seat, and that for nearly a quarter of a mile the animal had been dashing madly along uncontrolled. And then they understood that they had had a narrow escape from being killed.

A four-wheel cab-horse took fright about four years ago near Hyde Park Corner, and after a short but exciting run crashed into an omnibus. The cab was damaged, and one of the omnibus horses received a bad cut. The wounded animal was taken at once to a veterinary surgeon, who examined the wound as thoroughly as the blood would permit and then sewed it up. But it did not heal as quickly as he expected, and when three or four weeks had expired he became convinced that there was some foreign matter in the wound. So he opened it, and discovered, deeply embedded in the flesh, the whole of one of the cab-door handles, for which cabby had made a fruitless search soon after the accident.

# CHAPTER VII

The Shrewsbury and Talbot cabs—The Court hansom—The Parlour four-seat hansom—Electric cabs introduced—The "taxameter"—Empty cabs—Number of cabs in London—Cab fares—Two-horse cabs.

FROM the introduction of hansoms and clarences until 1897, no new cab of any importance was licensed. There were, however, several improved hansoms placed upon the streets. The most important of these was Earl Shrewsbury and Talbot's indiarubber-tyred Forder-built cab, which was introduced about 1880. In every respect the Shrewsbury and Talbot cabs were superior to any others plying for hire, and their popularity was assured from the first. Each of these cabs had S.T. surmounted by a coronet painted above the side windows, and, as the wheels were noiseless, small bells were placed on the horse.

But although Lord Shrewsbury and Talbot raised the standard of London cabs, and thereby earned the gratitude of the travelling public, he is not regarded with friendly feelings by other cab proprietors. They, or the majority of them, declare that he ruined the cab trade. When the Shrewsbury and Talbot cabs started work it became necessary for other proprietors to have indiarubber tyres on their vehicles—an expense which they grudged, as, being prevented by law from increasing the fares, they saw no prospect of getting back their money.

In June, 1888, the Shrewsbury and Talbot Cab and Noiseless Tyre Company, Limited, was formed, "to purchase, amalgamate, and carry on (1) the business of a cab proprietor and job-master worked by the Right Honourable the Earl of Shrewsbury and Talbot, and (2) the business of manufacturers of steel and rubber tyres carried on by the Noiseless Tyre Company, Limited, in Manchester and London."

Other variations of the hansom were the "court" and the "parlour." The court-hansom is a four-wheeler with accommodation for two people, and the driver's seat is in the same position as in an ordinary hansom. They are not numerous, but those that are plying for hire appear to be well patronised.

In January, 1887, the "parlour four-seat hansom," patented by Mr. Joseph Parlour, was announced as about to be placed on the streets. It was a very novel hansom. The driver sat at the back, with a sliding door on either side of him,

PARLOUR'S HANSOM.

which he could open or close with ease, permitting the riders to step from the vehicle on to the kerb. Passengers sat face to face, two on each side. A hansom with a sliding roof, and another with a movable hood, have also been tried in London.

One of the most important events in cab history

occurred in 1897. For more than a century English people, strong in their belief that Mother Shipton's prophecy would be fulfilled, have regarded with great interest every attempt to invent horseless carriages. As long ago as 1771 our very good friend the horse was threatened with elimination, if not extinction, and pictures of superannuated and disconsolate horses gazing over a hedge at horseless vehicles careering along the road, to the evident enjoyment of the riders, were almost as plentiful as they were four years ago. In 1771 a horseless carriage, invented by a mathematical instrument maker, had a trial run in the Artillery ground near the Minories. The event aroused the greatest interest, and the failure of the vehicle to realise the expectations formed of it by no means disheartened the horseless carriage enthusiasts. They declared that before long a reliable horseless carriage would certainly be invented. In 1790 there was a belief that their prophecy had been fulfilled, for invitations were sent out to members of the Society of Arts, engineers, and all interested in mechanics and vehicular traffic to attend a certain place on a stated day to inspect a horseless carriage, which possessed the additional novelty of having one wheel only. A large proportion of the invitations were accepted, and when the expectant people had assembled, their host, with great ceremony, led them to the coach-house and showed them the one-wheeled horseless vehicle—a wheel-barrow!

After that incident, which was talked about all over England—much to the disgust of the members of the Society of Arts who had attended the private view—the interest in horseless vehicle invention subsided for more than thirty years. When at last the craze did again break out, cabs appear to have been overlooked. Steam barouches, vans and omnibuses were invented in large numbers, but no one appears to have tried his hand at a steam cab, and it was not until 1897 that horseless cabs were placed on the London streets. These electric cabs were a pleasing novelty to Londoners and were well patronised, but it must be confessed that there were several objections to them. The want of originality in their build was very marked, for in appearance, although they only carried two passengers, they differed but little from a four-wheeler minus the horse and shafts. But that is a trivial objection compared with the following one which concerned the safety of the public. There are many people living who have been knocked down by carriages, cabs, omnibuses and vans, and have suffered little or no injury because they happened, by chance or design, to roll under the vehicle and thus escaped all four wheels. But if knocked down by one of the electric cabs no such escape

ELECTRIC CAB.

would have been possible, as the accumulator was only a few inches from the ground, and would have crushed to death any one who got beneath it.

Many of our public vehicles are very badly lighted, but no such complaint could be made against the electric cabs. They were, perhaps, a little too brilliantly illuminated for the comfort of people of a bashful disposition, who were worried by the thought that as they rode along they were as conspicuous as if they were on the stage with the limelight turned on them. If a man desired to ride through the streets at night unobserved, he did not hire an electric cab. And it does not follow that because a man wishes to escape notice that he is ashamed of being seen. But, as before stated, the electric cabs, or "humming birds," as they were named by the cabmen, were well patronised while on the streets, and certainly it was not for want of support that they were withdrawn. Those indiarubber tyres which so constantly needed attention were no doubt the cause of their withdrawal.

Barely had the electric cabs disappeared than an innovation was made which, in years to come, will be considered one of the most important events in the history of London cabs. On March 15, 1899, six cabs fitted with a distance registering apparatus, named the "taxameter," started from the Hôtel Cecil on trial runs into different parts of London, and on the following day they were plying for hire in the streets, the drivers conspicuous with white silk hats. The taxameter is a small species of clock fixed on the outside of the right-hand window of the cab, and records at the end of every journey the distance travelled and the legal fare which the passenger has to pay, whether he has hired the cab by time or distance. It also registers extras paid for luggage and waiting, the number of journeys made, the number of miles travelled, and the total earnings of the day. When the cab is empty, a little red flag, which can be seen from a distance, projects from the side. Immediately a fare enters the cab the driver turns down a lever, which lowers the red flag and causes the words "not engaged" to disappear and be replaced by the tariff. When the end of the journey is reached the cabman pulls up the lever, and the distance travelled and the fare to be paid appears on the dial.

The cabmen were to be paid a wage of £2 2*s*. for a week of six days and a percentage on the earnings, and evidently there were many men who would have been glad to work on those terms, for in answer to the Taxameter Syndicate's advertisement for six drivers, three hundred men applied. By the public and the press the taxameter was received with the warmest approval, for it promised a check on the extortion, and abuse accompanying it when practised on women, which has of late become painfully common among some London cabmen, and has earned for them a notoriety which will take many years to live down. Women can travel in London by train, tram, omnibus and boat without fear of extortion and incivility, but they know from bitter experience, that every time they hire a cab they are running a risk of being cheated and afterwards abused for daring to utter a protest. Women, therefore, were naturally very pleased when they heard of the new check, but their joy was short-lived, for the Cab-drivers' Union interfered, and declared that any man who drove a taxameter cab was a "black-leg." The reasons given for this decision were by no means satisfactory, and the only conclusion that an unbiassed person can arrive at is, that the majority of cabmen, in spite of their constant complaints about their difficulty of earning a living, made, partly by overcharging, considerably more than the £2 2*s.* a-week and percentage of earnings offered by the Taxameter Syndicate. As the drivers would not take out taxameter cabs, the proprietors were compelled to remove the register from them. But the taxameter is far too useful an innovation to be suppressed at the word of the Cab-drivers' Union. The public must remember that the taxameter gives them the protection for which they have been sighing for years, and that if they are determined to enjoy its benefits the Cab-drivers' Union is powerless to prevent the boon. It may order a strike, but the spectacle of men refusing to work because they are not allowed to overcharge their customers will be more novel than edifying. Let us hope, however, that the cabmen will not be so foolish as to think of striking, but will recognise that the taxameter is bound to come into general use, and when it is again tried will accept the innovation with a good grace.

The taxameter was tried first in 1894 on a few cabs in Berlin, and met with considerable opposition from both cab proprietors and drivers. But the public appreciated the innovation, and patronised those cabs which had the register to such an extent that the opposition was overcome quickly, and soon 5500 of the 8000 cabs plying for hire in Berlin were fitted with the taxameter. In Hamburgh, Vienna, Dresden, Stockholm and numerous other Continental cities the taxameter is in use, and growing in public favour. It is also at work, or has been tried, in Manchester, Leeds, Liverpool and Bradford, and it will be strange indeed if in the course of a few years every public cab in London and the Provinces is not fitted with it.

On Queen Victoria's eightieth birthday electric cabs were placed once more on the streets. But in appearance they had not been altered for the better. The original cabs were painted tastefully in two colours, the upper part black and the lower part yellow, but the new ones were black entirely. Moreover, the new cabs were taller than the original ones, and the added inches gave them a clumsy appearance. The accumulator was, as in the previous cabs, only a few inches from the ground. After plying for hire for a few weeks they were taken off the streets and have not yet reappeared.

The electric cab that is to be an all-round success has not yet been invented, but experience is being bought, and it will be strange if we have to wait long for it. But that it will ever supersede entirely the horse-drawn hansom is far from being likely, for while you meet hundreds of people who have had one ride in an electric cab, you come across very few who have had two. It is not because their experience was unpleasant that they have not had a second one, but because it was not so enjoyable as a ride in a horse-drawn cab. Apparently the hansom cab has every prospect of retaining its popularity for another sixty years.

But, in spite of the hansom's popularity, Londoners had complained for a considerable period of the obstruction caused by empty hansoms crawling along the streets plying for hire. Throughout the day a long string of such vehicles, with here and there a four-wheeler, perambulated the Strand and Piccadilly, blocking the traffic and making it exceedingly difficult and somewhat dangerous for pedestrians to cross the road. In 1899 the police authorities put an end to the nuisance by issuing instructions that no empty cabs were to be allowed to proceed along the Strand or Piccadilly, but were to remain on the ranks in, or adjoining, those thoroughfares. The cabmen protested strongly against this regulation, but the public approved of it, for the traffic became much less congested. Moreover, as additional ranks were provided, the cabmen did not suffer from the alteration.

Some people declare that there are too many cabs on the streets, but it is certain that there are no more than the public require. If they were not patronised to an extent which makes them profitable to the proprietors and the drivers, they would not be plying for hire. On December 31, 1900, there were 11,252 licensed cabs in London, of which 7531 were two-wheelers and 3721 four-wheelers. There were 13,201 cab-drivers and 2782 proprietors. For each cab a proprietor pays £2 for a police licence, which has to be renewed 12 months after issue, and 15*s.* to the Inland Revenue on the first day of every year. The driver pays 5*s.* for his licence, which is renewable 12 months from the day of issue.

At the present day the fares are :—

BY DISTANCE.

| | *s.* | *d.* |
|---|---|---|
| If hired and discharged *within* the four-mile radius, for any distance not exceeding two miles ... ... | 1 | 0 |
| For every additional mile or part of a mile ... ... | 0 | 6 |
| If hired *outside* the four-mile radius, wherever discharged, for the first and each succeeding mile or part of a mile ... ... ... ... ... ... ... | 1 | 0 |
| If hired *within*, but discharged *outside* the radius, whole distance not exceeding one mile ... ... ... | 1 | 0 |
| But exceeding one mile, then for each mile ended *within* the radius 6*d.*, and for each mile or part of a mile *outside* ... ... ... .. ... ... | 1 | 0 |

### By Time.

| | s. | d. |
|---|---|---|
| Within the four-mile radius. Four-wheeled cabs for one hour or less .. ... ... ... ... | 2 | 0 |
| Two-wheeled cab ... ... ... ... ... | 2 | 6 |
| For every additional quarter of an hour or part of a quarter, four-wheelers ... ... ... ... | 0 | 6 |
| Two-wheelers ... ... ... ... ... ... | 0 | 8 |
| Four-wheelers, or two-wheelers, if hired *outside* the radius, wherever discharged, for one hour or less ... | 2 | 6 |
| If above one hour, then for every quarter of an hour or less ... ... ... ... ... ... ... | 0 | 8 |

If hired *within*, but discharged outside the radius, the fares are according to the two preceding paragraphs.

### Luggage.

| | s. | d. |
|---|---|---|
| For each package carried outside the vehicle ... ... | 0 | 2 |

### Additional Persons.

| | s. | d. |
|---|---|---|
| For each person above two (two children under ten years of age are reckoned as one person) ... ... | 0 | 6 |
| For a child under ten years of age, carried with two or more persons ... ... ... ... ... | 0 | 3 |

### Waiting.

| | s. | d. |
|---|---|---|
| By distance only. For every fifteen minutes completed, if hired *within* the four-mile radius : Four-wheelers | 0 | 6 |
| Two-wheelers ... ... ... ... ... ... | 0 | 8 |
| When hired *outside* the radius, four- or two-wheelers ... | 0 | 8 |

Unless stated to the cabman at the time of

hiring that he is engaged by time, fares must be paid according to distance. A driver can refuse to be hired by time between 8 p.m. and 6 a.m.

A cabman hired by distance must, unless prevented by the traffic, drive at the rate of six miles an hour; if hired by time, four miles an hour. Should he be requested to drive above the latter speed, he may demand, in addition to the time fare, for every mile, or any part of one, exceeding four miles, the fare regulated by distance.

There are no two-horse cabs plying for hire at the present day, but if there were the fares, according to an Act of Parliament of 1853, not yet repealed, would be 8*d.* for a mile or less distance, and 2*s.* 8*d.* for an hour or any portion of one. During the great snowstorm of January, 1881, when for several days the roads were impassable for omnibuses, a large number of cabs appeared with two horses—the hansoms' being harnessed tandem fashion. The drivers were well aware of the Act of 1853, and, in case any passenger should possess a knowledge of it, they took the precaution, before starting on a journey, to extract a promise from the rider that he would pay double the usual fare. That was reasonable, for, apart from the fact that vehicles were few and travelling difficult, the cabmen, by using two horses, were only able to be at work for half their customary time.

THE END